LIFE AND REMARKABLE
ADVENTURES OF ISRAEL R. POTTER

"Shortly after his return in infirm old age to his native land, a little narrative of his adventures, forlornly published on sleazy gray paper, appeared among the peddlers, written, probably not by himself, but taken down from his lips by another. But like the crutch-marks of the cripple by the Beautiful Gate, this blurred record is now out of print."

So Herman Melville, on June 17th, 1854, described this original volume in the Dedication (*To His Highness, The Bunker Hill Monument*) of his fictionalized version of Potter's autobiography.

The present edition is a faithful republication of Potter's own story, reset from the Henry Trumbull printing in 1824. The reproduction of the original title page and frontispiece illustration are from a copy in the New York Public Library and used with their kind permission. Also reproduced is the title page and frontispiece illustration of the J. Howard printing in the same year.

In an Appendix, the final chapters of Herman Melville's *Israel Potter* have been reproduced from the 1855 first edition printing.

D1303350

LIFE

and

REMARKABLE ADVENTURES

of

ISRAEL R. POTTER

Introduction by Leonard Kriegel

The American Experience Series

CONSULTING EDITOR: HENRY BAMFORD PARKES

CORINTH BOOKS
NEW YORK

LEONARD KRIEGEL is an Instructor of English at The
City College of New York. He has edited a book on the
political philosophy of the Founding Fathers which is soon
to be published and has written a number of stories and
articles.

Library of Congress Catalog Card No. 62-10046

THE AMERICAN EXPERIENCE SERIES

Published by Corinth Books Inc.
32 West Eighth Street, New York 11, N. Y.

Distributed by The Citadel Press
222 Park Avenue South, New York 3, N. Y.

Printed in the U.S.A.

NOBLE OFFSET PRINTERS, INC.
NEW YORK 3, N. Y.

INTRODUCTION

The Life and Remarkable Adventures of Israel Potter has been read, when it has been read at all, in the same way as college sophomores studying Shakespeare read *Plutarch's Lives,* not for the moral homilies of a great biographer but rather as notes for the study of *Julius Caesar* or *Antony and Cleopatra.* In the case of Israel Potter's *Life,* however, such an approach can at least be partially justified, since its primary significance remains as a source for Herman Melville's "Revolutionary narrative of a beggar." That Melville was unable to mold the source to fit his artistic conception becomes readily apparent when we read these memoirs for ourselves and then turn to his novel. Only after making such a comparison does one realize the truth of F. O. Matthiessen's assertion that for Melville, by the time he wrote *Israel Potter,* tragedy "had become so real that it could not be written." But despite his artistic failure, Melville's choice of subject remains interesting, both for what it tells us about Melville's deepening sense of despair and for what it tells us about individualism and democracy. For in these ghostwritten memoirs, a pensioner's plea to the government by "one of the few survivors who fought and bled for American Independence," Melville caught a striking reflection of his own state of mind. The real Israel Potter, like Melville's "Revolutionary beggar," was another name added to the long list of the world's victims. And it is as a victim that this "plebian Lear" speaks to us, too.

Not only is Israel a victim, he is—and for Melville's purposes this was most significant—an American victim. It is this quality, this peculiarly "frontier" attempt to reconcile the promise of life with the actualities of existence, that stamps the real Israel Potter. Somehow, for the American, life is never as good, as enobling, or as fulfilling as he feels it was meant to be. For against his dream of selfhood the American is forced to measure the accidental evil of existence itself. It was as such a gauge that Melville attempted to make use of this short *Life* of an insignificant "native of Cranston, Rhode Island." Despite his artistic failure, his instinct was undoubtedly sound. For Israel Potter is not merely another good man adrift in a world devoid of goodness: he is, above all, an American, whose ideals and aims are derived from that same self-reliant democratic ethos which Whitman and Emerson were later to celebrate. Hired laborer, farmer, chain bearer, hunter, trapper, Indian trader, merchant sailor, whaler, soldier, courier, spy, carpenter, and beggar, through it all, Israel remains the American, the man who, even in the hardships of exile, insists that all will be well once he can again walk "on American ground."

As it proved to be with so many of his countrymen, success was Israel's failure. He returned, in May, 1823, after an absence of 48 years, to an America that was already far different from the country he remembered leaving at the age of 31. He had grown older and now he looked back; America, too, had grown older, but now it looked forward. Israel had come home to die; America was far too busy in the conquest of itself to give death anything more than the platitudinous comfort of words. Israel petitioned the government for a pension; but the government was now stable, a government of laws and not of

men, and so his petition was rejected. After his long
exile Israel had come to understand that there were boundaries to any existence; American optimism made even
the recognition of such boundaries an impossibility.

Melville, to his credit, saw all of this. That he was not
able to integrate such insights into the novel that evolved
from these memoirs is not overly important; one year
after the publication of *Israel Potter*, he quit work on his
uncompleted philosophical novel, *The Confidence Man*,
which, despite its manifold faults, must be read as a
savage indictment of the shallow humanitarianism against
which the real Israel Potter proved to be so helpless. It
was in this novel that Melville provided his nihilistic
answer to the fragile, confused optimism with which Israel
attempted to confront living.

The differences between what Melville saw in Israel's
life and what Israel himself saw are interesting enough:
for Melville, who saw the truth so intensely that he found
himself unable to commit his perceptions to paper, Israel's
life was further proof of man's insignificance in a universe
whose order remains completely beyond his comprehen-
sion; but Israel, who is neither what Madison Avenue or
Socrates calls a "thinking man," constantly confuses the
what is of life with the *what ought to be*. One sees the
limitations of Israel's perception in his attitude towards
Benjamin Franklin; Israel praises Franklin as "that great
and good man," the living embodiment of all that the
American dream promises. For Melville, on the other
hand, Franklin is not the embodiment but the decay of
that dream, the sophisticated but soulless statesman who
is damned as "everything but a poet." The real Israel dis-
misses Franklin in two pages, but Melville cannot dismiss
him for six chapters. "It's wisdom that's cheap, and it's

fortune that's dear," Melville has his Israel say as he dis-
gustedly slams down a copy of *Poor Richard*. But the real
Israel was a believer in wisdom; wisdom, along with goodness and self-reliance and Christianity, was the way to
fortune. And it is because of this lack of perception that
his own story is a far truer portrayal of the mystique of
victimization than is Melville's novel. Israel consistently
does the admirable thing at the right time, only to see
himself mocked by circumstance or fate or whatever label
we choose to give to the quiet terror that life so frequently
breeds.

Perhaps it was also his limited perception that enabled
Israel to devote almost half these memoirs to his years of
exile; he records his sufferings in detail, a record that was
so painful to Melville that he could do no more than hur-
riedly outline it in a few short, concluding chapters. One
can scarcely see what other choice Melville could have
made—such intense and unalleviated suffering can easily
make of its victim a mock-epic buffoon. In his own story,
Israel manages to avoid this fate, but only because he
does not fully understand what is happening to him. Melville saw the truth; because it was so painful, however,
he found himself unable to write it.

The Life and Remarkable Adventures of Israel Potter
was published in Providence in 1824, one year after Israel
"succeeded in the (79th year of his age) in obtaining a passage to his native country after an absence of 48 years."
This small book, written and published by Henry Trumbull, a Providence, Rhode Island printer, did not help him
achieve his objective: his quest for a pension proved un-
successful, and he died soon after, on "the same day,"
Melville tells us, "that the oldest oak in his native hills
was blown down." He took with him whatever was left

of his dream and his pride, an end which, to some extent, all victims share. "Kings as clowns," Melville wrote bitterly, "are codgers—who ain't a nobody?" It is a fitting epitaph for all the Israel Potters.

LEONARD KRIEGEL
The City College of New York

"OLD CHAIRS TO MEND"

ISRAEL R. POTTER,

Born in Cranston (Rhode Island) August 1st. 1744.

LIFE

AND

REMARKABLE ADVENTURES

OF

ISRAEL R. POTTER,

(A NATIVE OF CRANSTON, RHODE-ISLAND,)

WHO WAS A SOLDIER IN THE

AMERICAN REVOLUTION,

And took a distinguished part in the Battle of Bunker
Hill (in which he received three wounds,) after
which he was taken Prisoner by the British, conveyed to England, where for 30 years he obtained a
livelihood for himself and family, by crying "*Old
Chairs to Mend,*" through the Streets of London.—
In May last, by the assistance of the American Consul, he succeeded (in the 79th year of his age) in
obtaining a passage to his native country, after an
absence of 48 years.

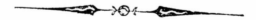

PROVIDENCE:
Printed by J. HOWARD, for I. R. POTTER—1824.
(Price 31 Cents.)

"OLD CHAIRS TO MEND?"

ISRAEL R. POTTER

Born in Cranston R.I. August 1st 1744.

LIFE

AND

REMARKABLE ADVENTURES

OF

ISRAEL R. POTTER,

(A NATIVE OF CRANSTON, RHODE-ISLAND.)

WHO WAS A SOLDIER IN THE

AMERICAN REVOLUTION,

And took a distinguished part in the Battle of Bunker Hill (in which he received three wounds.) after which he was taken Prisoner by the British, conveyed to England, where for 30 years he obtained a livelihood for himself and family, by crying " *Old Chairs to Mend*" through the Streets of London.— In May last, by the assistance of the American Consul, he succeeded (in the 79th year of his age) in obtaining a passage to his native country, after an absence of 48 years.

PROVIDENCE:
Printed by HENRY TRUMBULL—1824.
(Price 28 Cents.)

PREFACE.

IN the foregoing pages we have attempted a simple narrative of the life and extraordinary adventures of one of the few survivors who fought and bled for American Independence. There is not probably another now living who took an equally active part in the Revolutionary war, whose life has been marked with more extraordinary events, and who has drank deeper of the cup of adversity, than the aged veteran with whose History we now beg liberty to present the American public. Doomed by the fate of War to be early separated from kindred and friends, and to be conveyed by a foreign foe a prisoner of war from his native land, to a far distant country, where after having for 48 years experienced almost every hardship and deprivation of which adverse fortune is productive, providence appears at length to have so far interfered in his behalf, as to provide means whereby he has been enabled at an advanced age once more to visit and inhale the pure air of his native land. At the age of Seventy-Nine, an age in which it cannot be expected that the lamp of human life can long remain unextinguished, he has arrived among us, in a state of penury and want, to seek in common with his countrymen the enjoyment of a few of the blessings produced by American valour, in her memorable conflict with the mother country and in which he took a distinguished part.

As it yet remains doubtful whether (in consequence of his long absence) he will be so fortunate as to be included in that number to whom Government has granted pensions for their Revolutionary services, it is to obtain if possible a humble pittance as a remuneration, in part, for the unprecedented privations and sufferings of which he has been the unfortunate subject, that he is now induced to present the public with the following concise and simple narration of the most extraordinary incidents of his life.

LIFE AND ADVENTURES

OF

ISRAEL R. POTTER,

———

I WAS born of reputable parents in the town of Cranston, State of Rhode Island, August 1st, 1744. —I continued with my parents there in the full enjoyment of parental affection and indulgence, until I arrived at the age of 18, when, having formed an acquaintance with the daughter of a Mr. Richard Gardner, a near neighbour, for whom (in the opinion of my friends) entertaining too great a degree of partiality, I was reprimanded and threatened by them with more severe punishment, if my visits were not discontinued. Disappointed in my intentions of forming an union (when of suitable age) with one whom I really loved, I deemed the conduct of my parents in this respect unreasonable and oppressive, and formed the determination to leave them, for the purpose of seeking another home and other friends.

It was on Sunday, while the family were at meeting, that I packed up as many articles of my cloathing as could be contained in a pocket handkerchief, which, with a small quantity of provision, I conveyed to and secreted in a piece of woods in the rear of my father's house; I then returned and continued in the house until about 9 in the evening, when with the pretence of retiring to bed, I passed into a back room and from thence out of a back door and hastened to the spot where I had deposited my cloathes, &c.—it was a warm summer's night, and that I might be enabled to travel with the more facility the succeeding day, I lay down at the foot of a tree and reposed myself until about 4 in the morning when I arose and commenced my journey, travelling westward, with an intention of reaching if possible the new countries, which I had heard highly spoken of as affording excellent prospects for industrious and enterprising young men—to evade the pursuit of my friends, by whom I knew I should be early missed and diligently sought for, I confined my travel to the woods and shunned the public roads, until I had reached the distance of about 12 miles from my father's house.

At noon the succeeding day I reached Hartford, in Connecticut, and applied to a farmer in that town for work, and for whom I agreed to labour for one month for the sum of six dollars. Having completed my month's work to the satisfaction of my employer, I received my money and started from Hartford for Otter Creek; but, when I reached Springfield, I met with a man bound to the Cahos country, and who offered me four dollars to accompany him, of which offer I accepted, and the next morning we left Springfield and in a canoe ascended Connecticut river, and in about two weeks after much hard labour in paddling and poling the boat against the current, we reached Lebanon (N. H.), the place of our destination. It was with some difficulty and not until I had procured a writ, by the assistance of a respectable innkeeper in Lebanon, by the name of Hill, that I obtained from my last employer the four dollars which he had agreed to pay me for my services.

From Lebanon I crossed the river to New-Hartford (then N. Y.) where I bargained with a Mr. Brink of that town for 200 acres of new land, lying in New Hampshire, and for which I was to labour for him four months. As this may appear to some a small consideration for so great a number of acres of land, it may be well here to acquaint the reader with the situation of the country in that quarter, at that early period of its settlement—which was an almost impenetrable wilderness, containing but few civilized inhabitants, far distantly situated from each other and from any considerable settlement; and whose temporary habitations with a few exceptions were constructed of logs in their natural state—the woods abounded with wild beasts of almost every description peculiar to this country, nor were the few inhabitants at that time free from serious apprehension of being at some unguarded moment suddenly attacked and destroyed, or conveyed into captivity by the savages, who from the commencement of the French war, had improved every favourable opportunity to cut off the defenceless inhabitants of the frontier towns.

After the expiration of my four months labour the person who had promised me a deed of 200 acres of land therefor, having refused to fulfill his engagements, I was obliged to engage with a party of his Majesty's Surveyors at fifteen shillings per month, as an assistant chain bearer, to survey the wild unsettled lands bordering on the Connecticut river, to its source. It was in the winter season, and the snow so deep that it was impossible to travel without snow shoes—at the close of each day we enkindled a fire, cooked our victuals and erected with the branches of hemlock a temporary hut, which served us for a shelter for the night. The Surveyors having completed their business returned to Lebanon, after an absence of about two months. Receiving my wages I purchased a fowling-piece and ammunition therewith, and for the four succeeding months devoted my time in hunting Deer, Beavers, &c. in which I was very successful, as in the four months I obtained as many skins of these animals as produced me forty dollars—with my money I purchased of a Mr. John Marsh, 100 acres of new land, lying on Water Quechy River (so called) about five miles from Hartford (N. Y.). On this land I went immediately to work, erected a small log hut thereon, and in two summers without any assistance, cleared up thirty acres fit for sowing—in the winter seasons I employed my time in hunting and entraping such animals whose hides and furs were esteemed of the most value. I remained in possession of my land two years, and then disposed of it to the same person of whom I purchased it, at the advanced price of 200 dollars, and then conveyed my skins and furs which I had collected the two preceding winters, to NO. 4 (now Charlestown), where I exchanged them for Indian blankets, wampeag and such other articles as I could conveniently convey on a hand sled, and with which I started for Canada, to barter with the Indians for furs.— This proved a very profitable trip, as I very soon disposed of every article at an advance of more than two hundred per cent, and received payment in furs at a reduced price, and for which I received in NO. 4, 200 dollars, cash. With this money, together with what I was before in possession of, I now set out for home, once more to visit my parents after an absence of two years and nine months, in which time my friends had not been enabled to receive any correct information of me. On my arrival, so greatly effected were my parents at the presence of a son whom they had considered dead, that it was sometime before either could become sufficiently composed to listen to or to request me to furnish them with an account of my travels.

Soon after my return, as some atonement for the anxiety which I had caused my parents, I presented them with most of the money that I had earned in my absence, and formed the determination that I would remain with them contented at home, in consequence of a conclusion from the welcome reception that I met with, that they had repented of their opposition, and had become reconciled to my intended union—but, in this, I soon found that I was mistaken; for, although overjoyed to see me alive, whom they had supposed really dead, no sooner did they find that my long absence had rather increased than diminished my attachment for their neighbor's daughter, than their resentment and opposition appeared to increase in proportion—in consequence of which I formed the determination again to quit them, and try my fortune at sea, as I had now arrived at an age in which I had an unquestionable right to think and act for myself.

After remaining at home one month, I applied for and procured a birth at Providence, on board the Sloop ——, Capt. Fuller, bound to Grenada—having completed her loading (which consisted of stone lime, hoops, staves, &c.) we set sail with a favourable wind, and nothing worthy of note occurred until the 15th day from that on which we left Providence, when the sloop was discovered to be on fire, by a smoke issuing from her hold—the hatches were immediately raised, but as it was discovered that the fire was caused by water communicating with the lime, it was deemed useless to make any attempts to extinguish it—orders were immediately thereupon given by the captain to hoist out the long boat, which was found in such a leaky condition as to require constant bailing to keep her afloat; we had only time to put on board a small quantity of bread, a firkin of butter and a ten gallon keg of water, when we embarked, eight in number, to trust ourselves to the mercy of the waves, in a leaky boat and many leagues from land. As our provision was but small in quantity, and it being uncertain how long we might remain in our perilous situation, it was proposed by the captain soon after leaving the sloop, that we should put ourselves on an allowance of one biscuit and half a pint of water per day, for each man, which was readily agreed to by all on board—in ten minutes after leaving the sloop she was in a complete blaze, and presented an awful spectacle. With a piece of the flying-jib, which had been fortunately thrown into the boat, we made shift to erect a sail, and proceeded in a southwest direction in hopes to reach the spanish maine, if not so fortunate as to fall in with some vessel in our course—which, by the interposition of kind providence in our favour, actually took place the second day after leaving the sloop—we were discovered and picked up by a Dutch ship bound from Eustatia to Holland, and from the captain and crew met with a humane reception, and were supplied with every necessary that the ship afforded—we continued on board one week when we fell in with an American sloop bound from Piscataqua to Antigua, which received us all on board and conveyed us in safety to the port of her destination. At Antigua I got a birth on board an American brig bound to Porto Rico, and from thence to Eustatia. At Eustatia I received my discharge and entered on board a Ship belonging to Nantucket, and bound on a whaling voyage, which proved an uncommonly short and successful one—we returned to Nantucket full of oil after an absence of the ship from that port of only 16 months. After my discharge I continued about one month on the island, and then took passage for Providence, and from thence went to Cranston, once more to visit my friends, with whom I continued three weeks, and then returned to Nantucket. From Nantucket I made another whaling voyage to the South Seas and after an absence of three years, (in which time I experienced almost all the hardships and deprivations peculiar to Whalemen in long voyages) I succeeded by the blessings of providence in reaching once more my native home, perfectly sick of the sea, and willing to return to the bush and exchange a mariner's life for one less hazardous and fatiguing.

I remained with my friends at Cranston a few weeks, and then hired myself to a Mr. James Water-

man, of Coventry, for 12 months, to work at farming. This was in the year 1774, and I continued
with him about six months, when the difficulties
which had for some time prevailed between the
Americans and Britons, had now arrived at that
crisis, as to render it certain that hostilities would
soon commence in good earnest between the two
nations; in consequence of which, the Americans at
this period began to prepare themselves for the
event—companies were formed in several of the
towns in New England, who received the appella-
tion of "minute men," and who were to hold themselves in readiness to obey the first summons of
their officers, to march at a moment's notice;—a
company of this kind was formed in Coventry, into
which I enlisted, and to the command of which
Edmund Johnson, of said Coventry, was appointed.

It was on a Sabbath morning that news was received of the destruction of the provincial stores at
Concord, and of the massacre of our countrymen
at Lexington, by a detached party of the British
troops from Boston: and I immediately thereupon
received a summons from the captain, to be prepared
to march with the company early the morning ensuing—and, although I felt not less willing to obey
the call of my country at a minute's notice, and to
face her foes, than did the gallant Putnam, yet, the
nature of the summons did not render it necessary
for me, like him, to quit my plough in the field; as

having the day previous commenced the ploughing of a field of ten or twelve acres, that I might not leave my work half done, I improved the sabbath to complete it.

By the break of day Monday morning I swung my knapsack, shouldered my musket, and with the company commenced my march with a quick step for Charlestown, where we arrived about sunset and remained encamped in the vicinity until about noon of the 16th June; when, having been previously joined by the remainder of the regiment from Rhode Island, to which our company was attached, we received orders to proceed and join a detachment of about 1000 American troops, which had that morning taken possession of Bunker Hill, and which we had orders immediately to fortify, in the best manner that circumstances would admit of.   We laboured all night without cessation and with very little refreshment, and by the dawn of day succeeded in throwing up a redoubt of eight or nine rods square.   As soon as our works were discovered by the British in the morning, they commenced a heavy fire upon us, which was supported by a fort on Copp's hill; we however (under the command of the intrepid Putnam) continued to labour like beavers until our breast-work was completed.

About noon, a number of the enemy's boats and barges, filled with troops, landed at Charlestown, and commenced a deliberate march to attack us— we were now harangued by Gen. Putnam, who re-

minded us, that exhausted as we were, by our incessant labour through the preceding night, the most
important part of our duty was yet to be performed,
and that much would be expected from so great a
number of excellent marksmen—he charged us to
be cool, and to reserve our fire until the enemy approached so near as to enable us to see the white of
their eyes—when within about ten rods of our works
we gave them the contents of our muskets, and
which were aimed with so good effect, as soon to
cause them to turn their backs and to retreat with a
much quicker step than with what they approached
us. We were now again harangued by "old
General Put," as he was termed, and requested by
him to aim at the officers, should the enemy renew
the attack—which they did in a few moments, with
a reinforcement—their approach was with a slow
step, which gave us an excellent opportunity to
obey the commands of our General in bringing
down their officers. I feel but little disposed to
boast of my own performances on this occasion,
and will only say, that after devoting so many
months in hunting the wild animals of the wilderness, while an inhabitant of New Hampshire, the
reader will not suppose me a bad or unexperienced
marksman, and that such were the fare shots which
the epauletted red coats presented in the two attacks,
that every shot which they received from me, I am
confident on another occasion would have produced
me a deer skin.

So warm was the reception that the enemy met with in their second attack, that they again found it necessary to retreat, but soon after receiving a fresh reinforcement, a third assault was made, in which, in consequence of our ammunition failing, they too well succeeded—a close and bloody engagement now ensued—to fight our way through a very considerable body of the enemy, with clubbed muskets (for there were not one in twenty of us provided with bayonets) were now the only means left us to escape;—the conflict, which was a sharp and severe one, is still fresh in my memory, and cannot be forgotten by me while the scars of the wounds which I then received, remain to remind me of it!—fortunately for me, at this critical moment, I was armed with a cutlass, which although without an edge, and much rust-eaten, I found of infinite more service to me than my musket—in one instance I am certain it was the means of saving my life—a blow with a cutlass was aimed at my head by a British officer, which I parried and received only a slight cut with the point on my right arm near the elbow, which I was then unconscious of, but this slight wound cost my antagonist at the moment a much more serious one, which effectually dis-*armed* him, for with one well directed stroke I deprived him of the power of very soon again measuring swords with a "yankee rebel!" We finally however should have been mostly cut off, and compelled to yield to a superiour and better equipped force, had not a body of three or four hundred Connecticut men formed a temporary breast work, with rails &c. and by which means held the enemy at bay until our main body had time to ascend the heights, and retreat across the neck;—in this retreat I was less fortunate than many of my comrades—I received two musket ball wounds, one in my hip and the other near the ankle of my left leg —I succeeded however without any assistance in reaching Prospect Hill, where the main body of the Americans had made a stand and commenced fortifying—from thence I was soon after conveyed to the Hospital in Cambridge, where my wounds were dressed and the bullet extracted from my hip by one of the Surgeons; the house was nearly filled with the poor fellows who like myself had received wounds in the late engagement, and presented a melancholly spectacle.

Bunker Hill fight proved a sore thing for the British, and will I doubt not be long remembered by them; while in London I heard it frequently spoken of by many who had taken an active part therein, some of whom were pensioners, and bore indelible proofs of American bravery—by them the Yankees, by whom they were opposed, were not unfrequently represented as a set of infuriated beings, whom nothing could daunt or intimidate: and who, after their ammunition failed, disputed the ground, inch by inch, for a full hour with clubbed muskets, rusty swords, pitchforks and billets of wood, against the British bayonets.

I suffered much pain from the wound which I received in my ankle, the bone was badly fractured and several pieces were extracted by the surgeon, and it was six weeks before I was sufficiently recovered to be able to join my Regiment quartered on Prospect Hill, where they had thrown up entrenchments within the distance of little more than a mile of the enemy's camp, which was full in view, they having entrenched themselves on Bunker Hill after the engagement.

On the 3d July, to the great satisfaction of the Americans, General WASHINGTON arrived from the south to take command—I was then confined in the Hospital, but as far as my observations could extend, he met with a joyful reception, and his arrival was welcomed by every one throughout the camp—the troops had been long waiting with impatience for his arrival as being nearly destitute of ammunition and the British receiving reinforcements daily, their prospects began to wear a gloomy aspect.

The British quartered in Boston began soon to suffer much from the scarcity of provisions, and General Washington took every precaution to prevent their gaining a supply—from the country all supplies could be easily cut off, and to prevent their receiving any from Tories, and other disaffected persons by water, the General found it necessary to equip two or three armed vessels to intercept them—among these was the brigantine Washington of 10 guns, commanded by Capt. Martindale,—as seamen at this time could not easily be obtained, as most of them had enlisted in the land service, permission was given to any of the soldiers who should be pleased to accept of the offer, to man these vessels—consequently myself with several others of the same regiment went on board of the Washington, then lying at Plymouth, and in complete order for a cruise.

We set sail about the 8th December, but had been out but three days when we were captured by the enemy's ship Foy, of 20 guns, who took us all out and put a prize crew on board the Washington—the Foy proceeded with us immediately to Boston bay where we were put on board the British frigate Tartar and orders given to convey us to England.—When two or three days out I projected a scheme (with the assistance of my fellow prisoners, 72 in number) to take the ship, in which we should undoubtedly have succeeded, as we had a number of resolute fellows on board, had it not been for the treachery of a renegade Englishman, who betrayed us—as I was pointed out by this fellow as the principal in the plot, I was ordered in irons by the Officers of the Tartar, and in which situation I remained until the arrival of the ship at Portsmouth (Eng.) when I was brought on deck and closely examined, but protesting my innocence, and what was very fortunate for me in the course of the examination, the person by whom I had been betrayed, having been proved a British deserter, his story was discredited and I was relieved of my irons.

to be a true blooded yankee, requested him to supply me at his expense with as much liquor as I should call for.

The house was thronged early in the evening by many of the "good and faithful subjects of King George," who had assembled to take a peep at the "yankee rebel," (as they termed me) who had so recently taken an active part in the rebellious war, than raging in his Majesty's American provinces—while others came apparently to gratify a curiosity in viewing, for the first time, an "American Yankee!" whom they had been taught to believe a kind of non descripts—beings of much less refinement than the ancient Britains, and possessing little more humanity than the Buccaneers.

As for myself I thought it best not to be reserved, but to reply readily to all their inquiries; for while my mind was wholly employed in devising a plan to escape from the custody of my keepers, so far from manifesting a disposition to resent any of the insults offered me, or my country, to prevent any suspicions of my designs, I feigned myself not a little pleased with their observations, and in no way dissatisfied with my situation. As the officer had left orders with the landlord to supply me with as much liquor as I should be pleased to call for, I felt determined to make my keepers merry at his expense, if possible, as the best means that I could adopt to effect my escape.

The loyal group having attempted in vain to irritate me, by their mean and ungenerous reflections, by one (who observed that he had frequently heard it mentioned that the yankees were extraordinary dancers), it was proposed that I should entertain the company with a jig! to which I expressed a willingness to assent with much feigned satisfaction, if a fiddler could be procured—fortunately for them, there was one residing in the neighbourhood, who was soon introduced, when I was obliged (although much against my own inclination) to take the floor —with the full determination, however that if John Bull was to be thus diverted at the expense of an unfortunate prisoner of war, uncle Jonathan should come in for his part of the sport before morning, by showing them a few *Yankee steps* which they then little dreamed of.

By my performances they were soon satisfied that in this kind of exercise, I should suffer but little in competition with the most nimble footed Britain among them nor would they release me until I had danced myself into a state of perfect perspiration; which, however, so far from being any disadvantage to me, I considered all in favour of my projected plan to escape—for while I was pleased to see the flowing bowl passing merrily about, and not unfrequently brought in contact with the lips of my two keepers, the state of perspiration that I was in, prevented its producing on me any intoxicating effects.

The evening having become now far spent and

the company mostly retiring, my keepers (who, to use a sailor's phrase I was happy to discover "half seas over") having much to my dissatisfaction furnished me with a pair of handcuffs spread a blanket by the side of their bed on which I was to repose for the night. I feigned myself very grateful to them for having humanely furnished me with so comfortable a bed, and on which I stretched myself with much apparent unconcern, and remained quiet about one hour, when I was sure that the family had all retired to bed. The important moment had now arrived in which I was resolved to carry my premeditated plan into execution, or die in the attempt—for certain I .was that if I let this opportunity pass unimproved, I might have cause to regret it when it was too late—that I should most assuredly be conveyed early in the morning back to the floating prison from which I had so recently escaped, and where I might possibly remain confined until America should obtain her independence, or the differences between Great-Britain and her American provinces were adjusted. Yet should I in my attempt to escape meet with more opposition from my keepers, than what I had calculated from their apparent state of inebriety, the contest I well knew would be very unequal—they were two full grown stout men, with whom (if they were assisted by no others) I should have to contend, handcuffed! but, after mature deliberation, I resolved that however hazardous the attempt, it should be made, and that immediately.

After remaining quiet, as I before observed, until I thought it probable that all had retired to bed in the house, I intimated to my keepers that I was under the necessity of requesting permission to retire for a few moments to the back yard; when both instantly arose and reeling toward me seized each an arm, and proceeded to conduct me through a long and narrow entry to the back door, which was no sooner unbolted and opened by one of them, than I tripped up the heels of both and laid them sprawling, and in a moment was at the garden wall seeking a passage whereby I might gain the public road—a new and unexpected obstacle now presented, for I found the whole garden enclosed with a smooth bricken wall, of the heighth of twelve feet at least, and was prevented by the darkness of the night from discovering an avenue leading therefrom—in this predicament, my only alternative was either to scale this wall handcuffed as I was, and without a moment's hesitation, or to suffer myself to be made a captive of again by my keepers, who had already recovered their feet and were bellowing like bullocks for assistance—had it not been a very dark night, I must certainly have been discovered and re-taken by them;—fortunately before they had succeeded in rallying the family, in groping about I met with a fruit tree situated within ten or twelve feet of the wall, which I ascended as expeditiously as possible, and by an extraordinary leap from the branches reached the top of the wall, and was in an instant on the opposite side. The coast being now clear, I ran to the distance of two or three miles, with as much speed as my situation would admit of;—my next object now was to rid myself of my handcuffs, which fortunately proving none of the stoutest, I succeeded in doing after much painful labour.

It was now as I judged about 12 o'clock, and I had succeeded in reaching a considerable distance from the Inn from which I had made my escape, without hearing or seeing any thing of my keepers, whom I had left staggering about in the garden in search of their "Yankee captive!"—it was indeed to their intoxicated state, and the extreme darkness of the night, that I imputed my success in evading their pursuit. —I saw no one until about the break of day, when I met an old man, tottering beneath the weight of his pick-ax, hoe and shovel, clad in tattered garments, and otherwise the picture of poverty and distress; he had just left his humble dwelling, and was proceeding thus early to his daily labour;—and as I was now satisfied that it would be very difficult for me to travel in the day time garbed as I was, in a sailor's habit, without exciting the suspicions of his Royal Majesty's pimps, who (I had been informed) were constantly on the look-out for deserters, I applied to the old man, miserable as he appeared, for a change of cloathing, offering those which I then wore for a suit of inferior quality and less value—this I was induced to do at that moment, as I thought that the proposal could be made with perfect safety, for whatever might have been his suspicions as to my motives in wishing to exchange my dress, I doubted not, that with an object of so much apparent distress, self-interest would prevent his communicating them.— The old man however appeared a little surprised at my offer, and after a short examination of my pea-jacket, trousers, &c. expressed a doubt whether I would be willing to exchange them for his "Church suit," which he represented as something worse for wear, and not worth half so much as those I then wore—taking courage however from my assurances that a change of dress was my only object, he deposited his tools by the side of a hedge, and invited me to accompany him to his house, which we soon reached and entered, when a scene of poverty and wretchedness presented, which exceeded every thing of the kind that I had ever before witnessed—the internal appearance of the miserable hovel, I am confident would suffer in a comparison with any of the meanest stables of our American farmers—there was but one room, in one corner of which was a bed of straw covered with a coarse sheet, and on which reposed his wife and five small children. I had heard much of the impoverished and distressed situation of the poor in England, but the present presented an instance of which I had formed no conception—little indeed did I then think that it would be my lot, before I should meet with an opportunity to return to my native country, to be placed in an infinitely worse situation! but, alas, such was my hard fortune!

The first garment presented by the poor old man, of his best, or "church suit," as he termed it, was a coat of very coarse cloth, and containing a number of patches of almost every colour but that of the cloth of which it was originally made—the next was a waistcoat and a pair of small cloathes, which appeared each to have received a bountiful supply of patches to correspond with the coat—the coat I put on without much difficulty, but the two other garments proved much too small for me, and when I had succeeded with considerable difficulty in putting them on, they set so taut as to cause me some apprehension that they might even stop the circulation of blood!—my next exchange was my buff cap for an old rusty large brimmed hat.

The old man appeared very much pleased with his bargain, and represented to his wife that he could now accompany her to church much more decently clad—he immediately tried on the pea-jacket and trousers, and seemed to give himself very little concern about their size, although I am confident that one leg of the trousers was sufficiently large to admit his whole body—but, however ludicrous his appearance, in his new suit, I am confident that it could not have been more so than mine, garbed as I was, like an old man of seventy!—From my old friend I learned the course that I must steer to reach London, the towns and villages that I should have to pass through, and the distance thereto, which was between 70 and 80 miles. He likewise represented to me that the country was filled with soldiers, who were on the constant look-out for deserters from the navy and army, for the apprehension of which they received a stipulated reward.

After enjoining it on the old man not to give any information of me, should he meet on the road any-one who should enquire for such a person, I took my leave of him, and again set out with a determination to reach London, thus disguised, if possible;—I trav-elled about 30 miles that day, and at night entered a barn in hopes to find some straw or hay on which to repose for the night, for I had not money sufficient to pay for a night's lodging at a public house, had I thought it prudent to apply for one—in my expecta-tion to find either hay or straw in the barn I was sad-ly disappointed, for I soon found that it contained not a lock of either, and after groping about in the dark in search of something that might serve for a substi-tute, I found nothing better than an undressed sheep-skin—with no other bed on which to repose my wea-ried limbs I spent a sleepless night; cold, hungry and weary, and impatient for the arrival of the morning's dawn, that I might be enabled to pursue my journey.

By break of day I again set out and soon found my-self within the suburbs of a considerable village, in passing which I was fearful there would be some risk of detection, but to guard myself as much as possible against suspicion, I furnished myself with a crutch, and feigning myself a cripple, hobbled through the town without meeting with any interruption. In two hours after, I arrived in the vicinity of another still more considerable village, but fortunately for me, at the moment, I was overtaken by an empty baggage waggon, bound to London—again feigning myself very lame, I begged of the driver to grant a poor cripple the indulgence to ride a few miles, to which he assenting, I concealed myself by lying prostrate on the bottom of the waggon, until we had passed quite through the village; when, finding the waggoner disposed to drive much slower than what I wished to travel, after thanking him for the kind disposition which he had manifested to oblige me, I quit the waggon, threw away my crutch and travelled with a speed, calculated to surprise the driver with so suddenly a recovery of the use of my legs—the reader will perceive that I had now become almost an adept at deception, which I would not however have so frequently practiced, had not self-preservation demanded it.

As I thought there would be in my journey to London, infinitely more danger of detection in passing through large towns or villages, than in confining myself to the country, I avoided them as much as possible; and as I found myself once more on the borders of one, apparently of much larger size than any that I had yet passed, I thought it most expedient to take a circuitous route to avoid it; in attempting which, I met with an almost insurmountable obstacle, that I little dreamed of—when nearly abreast of the town, I found my route obstructed by a ditch, of upwards of 19 feet in breadth, and of what depth I could not determine; as there was now no other alternative left me, but to leap this ditch, or to retrace my steps and pass through the town, after a moment's reflection I determined to attempt the former, although it would be attempting a fete of activity, that I supposed myself incapable of performing; yet, however incredible it may appear, I assure my readers that I did effect it, and reached the opposite side with dry feet!

I had now arrived within about 16 miles of London, when night approaching, I again sought lodgings in a barn; which containing a small quantity of hay, I succeeded in obtaining a tolerable comfortable night's rest. By the dawn of day I arose somewhat refreshed, and resumed my journey with the pleasing prospect of reaching London before night—but, while encouraged and cheered by these pleasing anticipations, an unexpected occurrence blasted my fair prospects—I had succeeded in reaching in safety a distance so great from the place where I had been last held a prisoner, and within so short a distance of London, the place of my destination, that I began to think myself so far out of danger, as to cause me to relax in a measure, in the precautionary means which I had made use of to avoid detection;—as I was passing through the town of Staines, (within a few miles of London) about 11 o'clock in the forenoon, I was met by three or four British soldiers, whose notice I attracted, and who unfortunately for me, discovered by the collar (which I had not taken the precaution to conceal) that I wore a shirt which exactly corresponded with those uniformly worn by his Majesty's seamen—not being able to give a satisfactory account of myself, I was made a prisoner of, on suspicion of being a deserter from his Majesty's service, and was immediately committed to the Round House; a prison so called, appropriated to the confinement of runaways, and those convicted of small offenses—I was committed in the evening, and to secure me the more effectually, I was handcuffed, and left supperless by my unfeeling jailor, to pass the night in wretchedness.

I had now been three days without food (with the exception of a single two-penny loaf) and felt myself unable much longer to resist the cravings of nature—my spirits, which until now had armed me with fortitude began to forsake me—indeed I was at this moment on the eve of despair! when, calling to mind that grief would only aggravate my calamity, I endeavoured to arm my soul with patience; and habituate myself as well as I could, to woe.—Accordingly I roused my spirits; and banishing for a few moments, these gloomy ideas, I began to reflect seriously, on the methods how to extricate myself from this labyrinth of horror.

My first object was to rid myself of my handcuffs, which I succeeded in doing after two hours hard labour, by sawing them across the grating of the window; having my hands now at liberty, the next thing to be done was to force the door of my apartment, which was secured on the outside by a hasp and padlock; I devised many schemes but for the want of tools to work with, was unable to carry them into execution—I however at length succeeded, with the assistance of no other instrument than the bolt of my handcuffs; with which, thrusting my arm through a small window or aperture in the door, I forced the padlock, and as there was now no other barrier to prevent my escape, after an imprisonment of about five hours, I was once more at large.

It was now as I judged about midnight, and although enfeebled and tormented with excessive hunger and fatigue, I set out with the determination of reaching London, if possible, early the ensuing morning. By break of day I reached and passed through Brintford, a town of considerable note and within six miles of the Capital—but so great was my hunger at this moment, that I was under serious apprehension of falling a victim to absolute starvation, if not so fortunate soon to obtain something to appease it. I recollected of having read in my youth, accounts of the dreadful effects of hunger, which had led men to the commission of the most horrible excesses, but did not then think that fate would ever thereafter doom me to an almost similar situation.

When I made my escape from the Prison ship, six English pennies was all the money that I possessed—with two I had purchased a two penny loaf the day after I had escaped from my keepers at the Inn, and the other four still remained in my possession, not having met with a favourable opportunity since the purchase of the first loaf to purchase food of any kind. When I had arrived at the distance of one and an half miles from Brintford, I met with a labourer employed in building a pale fence, to whom my deplorable situation induced me to apply for work; or for information of any one in the neighbourhood, that might be in want of a hand to work at farming or gardening. He informed me that he did not wish himself to hire, but that Sir John Miller, whose seat he represented but a short distance, was in the habit of employing many hands at that season of the year (which was in the spring of 1776) and he doubted not but that I might there meet with employment.

With my spirits a little revived, at even a distant prospect of obtaining something to alleviate my sufferings, I started in quest of the seat of Sir John, agreeable to the directions which I had received; in attempting to reach which, I mistook my way, and proceeded up a gravelled and beautifully ornamented walk, which unconsciously led me directly to the garden of the Princess Amelia—I had approached within view of the Royal Mansion when a glimpse of a number of "red coats" who thronged the yard, satisfied me of my mistake, and caused me to make an instantaneous and precipitate retreat, being determined not to afford any more of their mess an opportunity of boasting of the capture of a "Yankee Rebel,"—indeed, a wolf or a bear, of the American wilderness, could not be more terrified or panic-struck at the sight of a firebrand, than I then was at that of a British red coat!

Having succeeded in making good my retreat from the garden of her highness, without being discovered, I took another path which led me to where a number of labourers were employed in shovelling gravel, and to whom I repeated my enquiry if they could inform me of any in want of help, &c.—"why in troth friend (answered one in a dialect peculiar to the labouring class of people of that part of the country) me master, Sir John, hires a goodly many, and as we've a deal of work now, may-be he'll hire you; 'spose he stop a little with us until work is done, he may then gang along, and we'll question Sir John, whither him be wanting another like us or no!"

Although I was sensible that an application of this kind, might lead to a discovery of my situation, whereby I might be again deprived of my liberty, and immured in a loathsome prison; yet, as there was now no other alternative left me but to seek in this way, something to satisfy the cravings of hunger, or to yield a victim to starvation, with all its attending horrors: of the two evils I preferred the least, and concluded as the honest labourer had proposed, to await until they had completed their work, and then to accompany them home to ascertain the will of Sir John.

As I had heard much of the tyrannical and domineering disposition of the rich and purse-proud of England, and who were generally the lords of the manor, and the particular favourites of the crown; it was not without feeling a very considerable degree of diffidence, that I introduced myself into the presence of one whom I strongly suspected to be of that class—but, what was peculiarly fortunate for me, a short acquaintance was sufficient to satisfy me that as regarded this gentleman, my apprehensions were without cause. I found him walking in his front yard in company with several gentlemen, and on being made acquainted with my business, his first enquiry was whether I had a hoe, or money to purchase one, and on being answered in the negative, he requested me to call early the ensuing morning, and he would endeavour to furnish me with one.

It is impossible for me to express the satisfaction that I felt at this prospect of a deliverance from my wretched situation. I was now by so long fasting reduced to such a state of weakness, that my legs were hardly able to support me, and it was with extreme difficulty that I succeeded in reaching a baker's shop in the neighbourhood, where with my four remaining pennies, which I had reserved for a last resource, I purchased two two-penny loaves.

After four days of intolerable hunger, the reader may judge how great must have been my joy, to find myself in possession of even a morsel to appease it—well might I have exclaimed at this moment with the unfortunate Trenck—"O nature! what delight hast thou combined with the gratification of thy wants! remember this ye who rack invention to excite appetite, and which yet you cannot procure; remember how simple are the means that will give a crust of mouldy bread a flavour more exquisite than all the spices of the east, or all the profusion of land or sea; remember this, grow hungry, and indulge your sensuality."

Although five times the quantity of the "staff of life" would have been insufficient to have satisfied my appetite, yet, as I thought it improbable that I should be indulged with a mouthful of any thing to eat in the morning, I concluded to eat then but one loaf, and to reserve the other for another meal; but having eaten one, so far from satisfying, it seemed rather to increase my appetite for the other—the temptation was irresistable—the cravings of hunger predominated, and would not be satisfied until I had devoured the remaining one.

The day was now far spent and I was compelled to resort with reluctance to a carriage house, to spend another night in misery; I found nothing therein on which to repose my wearied limbs but the bare floor, which was sufficient to deprive me of sleep, however much exhausted nature required it; my spirits were however buoyed up by the pleasing consolation that the succeeding day would bring relief;—as soon as day light appeared, I hastened to await the commands of one, whom, since my first introduction, I could not but flatter myself would prove my benefactor, and afford me that relief which my pitiful situation so much required—it was an hour much earlier than that at which even the domestics were in the habit of arising, and I had been a considerable time walking back and forth in the barn yard, before any made their appearance. It was now about 4 o'clock, and by the person of whom I made the enquiry, I was informed that 8 o'clock was the usual hour in which the labourers commenced their day's work—permission was granted me by this person (who had the care of the stable) to repose myself on some straw beneath the manger, until they should be in readiness to depart to commence their day's work—in the four hours I had a more comfortable nap than any that I had enjoyed the four preceding nights. At 8 o'clock precisely all hands were called, and preparations made for a commencement of the labours of the day—I was furnished with a large iron fork and a hoe, and ordered by my employer to accompany them, and although my strength at this moment was hardly sufficient to enable me to bear even so light a burden, yet was unwilling to expose my weakness, so long as it could be avoided—but, the time had now arrived in which it was impossible for me any longer to conceal it, and had to confess the cause to my fellow labourers, so far as to declare to them, that such had been my state of poverty, that (with the exception of the four small loaves of bread) I had not tasted food for four days! I was not I must confess displeased nor a little disappointed to witness the evident emotions of pity and commiseration, which this woeful declaration appeared to excite in their minds: as I had supposed them too much accustomed to witness scenes of misery and distress, to have their feelings much effected by a brief recital of my sufferings and deprivations—but in justice to them I must say, that although a very illiterate, I found them (with a few exceptions) a humane and benevolent people.

About 11 o'clock we were visited by our employer, Sir John: who, noticing me particularly, and perceiving the little progress I made in my labour, observed, that although I had the appearance of being a stout hearty man, yet I either feigned myself or really was a very weak one! on which it was immediately observed by one of my friendly fellow labourers, that it was not surprising that I lacked strength, as I had eaten nothing of consequence for four days! Mr. Millet, who appeared at first little disposed to credit the fact, on being assured by me that it was really so, put a shilling into my hand, and bid me go immediately and purchase to that amount in bread and meat—a request which the reader may suppose I did not hesitate to comply with.

Having made a tolerable meal, and feeling somewhat refreshed thereby, I was on my return when I was met by my fellow labourers on their return home, four o'clock being the hour in which they usually quit work. As soon as we arrived, some victuals was ordered for me by Sir John, when the maid presenting a much smaller quantity, than what her benevolent master supposed sufficient to satisfy the appetite of one who had been four days fasting, she was ordered to return and bring out the platter and the whole of its contents, and of which I was requested to eat my fill, but of which I ate sparingly to prevent the dangerous consequences which might have resulted from my voracity in the debilitated state to which my stomach was reduced.

My light repast being over, one of the men were ordered by my hospitable friend to provide for me a comfortable bed in the barn, where I spent the night on a couch of clean straw, more sweetly than ever I had done in the days of my better fortune. I arose early much refreshed, and was preparing after breakfast to accompany the labourers to their work, which was no sooner discovered by Sir John, than smiling, he bid me return to my couch and there remain until I was in a better state to resume my labours; indeed the generous compassion and benevolence of this gentleman was unbounded. After having on that day partook of an excellent dinner, which had been provided expressly for me, and the domestics having been ordered to retire, I was not a little surprised to hear myself thus addressed by him—"my honest friend, I perceive that you are a sea-faring man, and your history probably is a secret which you may not wish to divulge; but, whatever circumstances may have attended you, you may make them known to me with the greatest safety, for I pledge my honour I will never betray you."

Having experienced so many proofs of the friendly disposition of Mr. Millet, I could not hesitate a moment to comply with his request, and without attempting to conceal a single fact, made him acquainted with every circumstance that had attended me since my first enlistment as a soldier—after expressing his regret that there should be any of his countrymen found so void of the principles of humanity, as to treat thus an unfortunate prisoner of war, he assured me that so long as I remained in his employ he would guarantee my safety—adding, that notwithstanding (in consequence of the unhappy differences which then prevailed between Great Britain and her American colonies) the inhabitants of the latter were denominated Rebels, yet they were not without their friends in England, who wished well to their cause, and would cheerfully aid them whenever an opportunity should present—he represented the soldiers (whom it had been reported to me, were constantly on the look out for deserters) as a set of mean and contemptible wretches, little better than a lawless banditti, who, to obtain the fee awarded by government, for the apprehension of a deserter, would betray their best friends.

Having been generously supplied with a new suit of cloathes and other necessaries by Mr. M. I contracted with him for six months, to superintend his strawberry garden, in the course of which so far from being molested, I was not suspected by even his own domestics of being an American—at the expiration of the six months, by the recommendation of my hospitable friend, I got a berth in the garden of the Princess Amelia, where although among my fellow labourers the American Rebellion was not unfrequently the topic of their conversation, and the "d--d Yankee Rebels" (as they termed them) frequently the subjects of their vilest abuse, I was little suspected of being one of that class whom they were pleased thus to denominate—I must confess that it was not without some difficulty, that I was enabled to surpress the indignant feelings occasioned by hearing my countrymen spoken so disrespectfully of, but as a single word in their favour might have betrayed me, I could obtain no other satisfaction than by secretly indulging the hope that I might before the conclusion of the war, have an opportunity to repay them, in their own coin, with interest.

I remained in the employ of the Princess about three months, and then in consequence of a misunderstanding with the overseer, I hired myself to a farmer in a small village adjoining Brintford, where I had not been three weeks employed before rumour was afloat that I was a Yankee Prisoner of war! from whence the report arose, or by what occasioned, I

never could learn—it no sooner reached the ears of
the soldiers, than they were on the alert, seeking an
opportunity to seize my person—fortunately I was
appraised of their intentions before they had time to
carry them into effect; I was however hard pushed,
and sought for by them with that diligence and per-
severance that certainly deserved a better cause—I
had many hair breadth escapes, and most assuredly
should have been taken, had it not been for the
friendship of those whom I suspect felt not less
friendly to the cause of my country, but dare not
publicly avow it—I was at one time traced by the
soldiers in pursuit of me to the house of one of this
description, in whose garret I was concealed, and was
at that moment in bed; they entered and enquired
for me, and on being told that I was not in the house,
they insisted on searching, and were in the act of
ascending the chamber stairs for that purpose, when
seizing my cloathes, I passed up through the scuttle,
and reached the roof of the house, and from thence
half naked passed to those of the adjoining ones to
the number of ten or twelve, and succeeded in making my escape without being discovered.

Being continually harassed by night and day by
the soldiers, and driven from place to place, without
an opportunity to perform a day's work, I was advised by one whose sincerity I could not doubt, to
apply for a berth as a labourer in a garden of his
Royal Majesty, situated in the village of Quew, a
few miles from Brintford; where, under the pro-

tection of his Majesty, it was represented to me that I should be perfectly safe, as the soldiers dare not approach the royal premises, to molest any one therein employed—he was indeed so friendly as to introduce me personally to the overseer, as an acquaintance who possessed a perfect knowledge of gardening, but from whom he carefully concealed the fact of my being an American born, and of the suspicion entertained by some of my being a prisoner of war, who had escaped the vigilance of my keepers.

The overseer concluded to receive me on trial; —it was here that I had not only frequent opportunities to see his Royal Majesty in person, in his frequent resorts to this, one of his country retreats, but once had the honour of being addressed by him. The fact was, that I had not been one week employed in the garden, before the suspicion of my being either a prisoner of war, or a Spy, in the employ of the American Rebels, was communicated, not only to the overseer and other persons employed in the garden, but even to the King himself! As I was one day busily engaged with three others in gravelling a walk, I was unexpectedly accosted by his Majesty: who, with much apparent good nature, enquired of me of what country I was—"an American born, may it please your Majesty," was my reply (taking off my hat, which he requested me instantly to replace on my head),— "ah! (continued he with a smile) an American, a stubborn, a very stubborn people indeed!—and what brought you to this country, and how long have you been here?" "the fate of war, your Majesty—I was brought to this country a prisoner about eleven months since,"—and thinking this a favourable opportunity to acquaint him with a few of my grievances, I briefly stated to him how much I had been harassed by the soldiers—"while here employed they will not trouble you," was the only reply he made, and passed on. The familiar manner in which I had been interrogated by his Majesty, had I must confess a tendency in some degree to prepossess me in his favour—I at least suspected him to possess a disposition less tyrannical, and capable of better view than what had been imputed to him; and as I had frequently heard it represented in America, that uninfluenced by such of his ministers, as unwisely disregarded the reiterated complaints of the American people, he would have been foremost to have redressed their grievances, of which they so justly complained.

I continued in the service of his Majesty's gardner at Quew, about four months, when the season having arrived in which the work of the garden required less labourers I with three others was discharged; and the day after engaged myself for a few months, to a farmer in the town and neighbourhood where I had been last employed—but, not one week had expired before the old story of my being an American prisoner of war &c. was revived and industriously circu-

lated, and the soldiers (eager to obtain the proffered
bounty) like a pack of blood-hounds were again on
the track seeking an opportunity to surprise me—
the house wherein I had taken up my abode, was
several times thoroughly searched by them, but I was
always so fortunate as to discover their approach in
season to make good my escape by the assistance of
a friend—to so much inconvenience however did
this continual apprehension and fear subject me,
that I was finally half resolved to surrender myself a
prisoner to some of his Majesty's officers, and submit
to my fate, whatever it might be, when by an unexpected occurrence, and the seasonable interposition
of providence in my favour, I was induced to change
my resolution.

I had been strongly of the opinion by what I had
myself experienced, that America was not without
her friends in England, and those who were her well
wishers in the important cause in which she was at
that moment engaged; an opinion which I think no
one will disagree with me in saying, was somewhat
confirmed, by a circumstance of that importance, as
entitles it to a conspicuous place in my narrative.
At a moment when driven almost to a state of
despondency by continual alarms and fears of falling
into the hands of a set of desperadoes, who for a very
small reward would willingly have undertaken the
commission of almost any crime; I received a message from a gentleman of respectability of Brintford
(J. Woodcock Esq.) requesting me to repair imme-

diately to his house—the invitation I was disposed to pay but little attention to, as I viewed it nothing more than a plan of my pursuers to decoy and entrap me—but, on learning from my confidential friend that the gentleman by whom the message had been sent, was one whose loyalty had been doubted, I was induced to comply with the request.

I reached the house of 'Squire Woodcock about 8 o'clock in the evening, and after receiving from him at the door assurances that I might enter without fear or apprehension of any design on his part against me, I suffered myself to be introduced into a private chamber, where were seated two other gentlemen, who appeared to be persons of no mean rank, and proved to be no other than Horne Tooke and James Bridges Esquires—as all three of these gentlemen have long since paid the debt of nature, and are placed beyond the reach of such as might be disposed to persecute or reproach them for their disloyalty, I can now with perfect safety disclose their names—names which ought to be dear to every true American.

After having (by their particular request) furnished these gentlemen with a brief account of the most important incidents of my life, I underwent a very strict examination, as they seemed determined to satisfy themselves, before they made any important advances or disclosures, that I was a person in whom they could repose implicit confidence. Finding me firmly attached to the interests of my country, so much so as to be willing to sacrifice even my life if necessary in her behalf, they began to address me with less reserve; and after bestowing the highest encomiums on my countrymen, for the bravery which they had displayed in their recent engagements with the British troops, as well as for their patriotism in publicly manifesting their abhorrence and detestation of the ministerial party in England, who to alienate their affections and to enslave them, had endeavoured to subvert the British constitution; they enquired of me if (to promote the interests of my country) I should have any objection to take a trip to Paris, on an important mission, if my passage and other expences were paid, and a generous compensation allowed me for my trouble; and which in all probability would lead to the means whereby I might be enabled to return to my country—to which I replied that I should have none. After having enjoined upon me to keep every thing which they had communicated, a profound secret, they presented me with a guinea, and a letter for a gentleman in White Waltam (a country town about 30 miles from Brintford) which they requested me to reach as soon as possible, and there remain until they should send for me, and by no means to fail to arrive at the precise hour that they should appoint.

After partaking of a little refreshment I set out at 12 o'clock at night, and reached White Waltam at half past 11 the succeeding day, and imme-

diately waited on and presented the letter to the
gentleman to whom it was directed, and who gave
me a very cordial reception, and whom I soon
found was as real a friend to America's cause as the
three gentlemen in whose company I had last been.
It was from him that I received the first information
of the evacuation of Boston by the British troops,
and of the declaration of INDEPENDENCE, by the
American Congress—he indeed appeared to possess a
knowledge of almost every important transaction in
America, since the memorable battle of Bunker-Hill,
and it was to him that I was indebted for many particulars, not a little interesting to myself, and which
I might otherwise have remained ignorant of, as I
have always found it a principle of the Britains, to
conceal every thing calculated to diminish or tarnish
their fame, as a "great and powerful nation!"

I remained in the family of this gentleman about
a fortnight, when I received a letter from 'Squire
Woodcock, requesting me to be at his house without fail precisely at 2 o'clock the morning ensuing—
in compliance of which I packed up and started immediately for Brintford, and reached the house of
'Squire Woodcock at the appointed hour—I found
there in company with the latter, the two gentlemen
whose names I have before mentioned, and by whom
the object of my mission to Paris was now made
known to me—which was to convey in the most secret
manner possible a letter to Dr. FRANKLIN; every
thing was in readiness, and a chaise ready harnessed

which was to convey me to Charing Cross, waiting at the door—I was presented with a pair of boots, made expressly for me, and for the safe conveyance of the letter of which I was to be the bearer, one of them contained a false heel, in which the letter was deposited, and was to be thus conveyed to the Doctor. After again repeating my former declarations, that whatever might be my fate, they should never be exposed, I departed, and was conveyed in quick time to Charing Cross, where I took the post coach for Dover, and from thence was immediately conveyed in a packet to Calais, and in fifteen minutes after landing, started for Paris; which I reached in safety, and delivered to Dr. Franklin the letter of which I was the bearer.

What were the contents of this letter I was never informed and never knew, but had but little doubt but that it contained important information relative to the views of the British cabinet, as regarded the affairs of America; and although I well knew that a discovery (while within the British dominions) would have proved equally fatal to me as to the gentlemen by whom I was employed, yet, I most solemnly declare, that to be serviceable to my country at that important period, was much more of an object with me, than the reward which I had been promised, however considerable it might be. My interview with Dr. Franklin was a pleasing one—for nearly an hour he conversed with me in the most agreeable and instructive manner, and listened to the tale of my sufferings with much apparent interest, and seemed disposed to encourage me with the assurance that if the Americans should succeed in their grand object, and firmly establish their Independence, they would not fail to remunerate their soldiers for their services —but, alas! as regards myself, these assurances have not as yet been verified!—I am confident, however, that had it been a possible thing for that great and good man (whose humanity and generosity have been the theme of infinitely abler pens than mine) to have lived to this day, I should not have petitioned my country in vain for a momentary enjoyment of that provision, which has been extended to so great a portion of my fellow soldiers; and whose hardships and deprivations, in the cause of their country, could not I am sure have been half so great as mine!

After remaining two days in Paris, letters were delivered to me by the Doctor, to convey to the gentlemen by whom I had been employed, and which for their better security as well as my own, I deposited as the other, in the heel of my boot, and with which to the great satisfaction of my friends I reached Brintford, in safety, and without exciting the suspicion of any one as to the important (although somewhat dangerous) mission that I had been engaged in. I remained secreted in the house of 'Squire Woodcock a few days, and then by his and the two other gentlemen's request, made a second trip to Paris, and in reaching which and in delivering my letters, was equally as fortunate as in my first. If I should succeed in returning in safety to Brintford this trip, I was (agreeable to the generous proposal of Doctor Franklin) to return immediately to France, from whence he was to procure me a passage to America; —but, although in my return I met with no difficulty, yet, as if fate had selected me as a victim to endure the miseries and privations which afterward attended me, but three hours before I reached Dover to engage a passage for the third and last time to Calais, all intercourse between the two countries was prohibited!

My flattering expectations of being enabled soon to return to my native country, and once more to meet and enjoy the society of my friends, (after an absence of more than twelve months) being thus by an unforeseen circumstance completely destroyed, I returned immediately to the gentlemen by whom I had been last employed to advise with them what it would be best for me to do, in my then unpleasant situation—for indeed, as all prospects were now at an end, of meeting with an opportunity very soon to return to America, I could not bear the idea of remaining any longer in a neighbourhood where I was so strongly suspected of being a fugitive from justice and under continual apprehension of being retaken, and immured like a felon in a dungeon.

By these gentlemen I was advised to repair immediately to London, where employed as a labourer, if I did not imprudently betray myself, they thought there was little probability of my being suspected of being an American. This advice I readily accepted as the plan was such a one as exactly accorded with my opinion, for from the very moment that I first escaped from the clutches of my captors, I thought that in the city of London I should not be so liable to be suspected and harassed by the soldiers, as I should to remain in the country. These gentlemen supplied me with money sufficient to defray my expenses and would have willingly furnished me with a recommendation had they not been fearful that if I should be so unfortunate as to be recognized by any one acquainted with the circumstance of my capture and escape, those recommendations (as their loyalty was already doubted) might operate much against them, in as much as they might furnish a clue to the discovery of some transactions which they then felt unwilling to have exposed. I ought here to state that before I set out for London, I was entrusted by these gentlemen with Five Guineas, which I was requested to convey and distribute among a number of Americans, then confined as prisoners of war, in one of the city prisons.

I reached London late in the evening and the next day engaged board at Five Shillings per week, at a public house in Lombard Street, where under a fictitious name I passed for a farmer from Lincolnshire —my next object was to find my way to the prison where were confined as prisoners of war a number of my countrymen, and among whom I was directed to distribute the 5 guineas with which I had been en-

trusted for that purpose by their friends at Brintford.
—I found the prison without much difficulty, but it
was with very considerable difficulty that I gained
admittance, and not until I had presented the turnkey
with a considerable fee would he consent to indulge
me. The reader will suppose that I must have been
very much surprised, when, as soon as the door of the
prisoner's apartment was opened, and I had passed
the threshold, to hear one of them exclaim with much
apparent astonishment, "Potter! is that you! how in
the name of heaven came you here!"—an exclamation
like this by one of a number to whom I supposed
myself a perfect stranger, caused me much uneasi-
ness for a few moments, as I expected nothing less
than to recognize in this man, some one of my old
shipmates, who had undoubtedly a knowledge of
the fact of my being a prisoner of war, and having
been confined as such on board the guard ship at spit-
head—but, in this I soon found to my satisfaction
that I was mistaken, for after viewing for a moment
the person by whom I had been thus addressed. I
discovered him to be no other than my old friend
seargent Singles, with whom I had been intimately
acquainted in America—as the exclamation was in
presence of the turnkey, least I should have the key
turned upon me, and be considered as lawful a prisoner as any of the rest, I hinted to my friend that
he certainly mistook me (a Lincolnshire farmer) for
another person, and by a wink which he received from
me at the same moment gave him to understand that

a renewal of our acquaintance or an exchange of civilities would be more agreeable to me at any other time. I now as I had been requested divided the money as equally as possible among them, and to prevent the suspicions of the keeper, I represented to them in a feigned dialect peculiar to the labouring people of the Shire-towns, that, "me master was owing a little trifle or so to a rebel trader of one of his Majesty's American provinces, and was quested by him to pay the ballance and so, to his brother yankee rebels here imprisoned."

I found the poor fellows (fifteen in number) confined in a dark filthy apartment of about 18 feet square; and which I could not perceive contained any thing but a rough plank bench of about 10 feet in length, and a heap of straw with one or two tattered, filthy looking blankets spread thereon, which was probably the only bedding allowed them—although their situation was such as could not fail to excite my pity, yet, I could do no more than lament that it was not in my power to relieve them—how long they remained thus confined or when exchanged, I could never learn, as I never to my knowledge saw one of them afterwards.

For four or five days, after I reached London, I did very little more than walk about the city, viewing such curiosities as met my eye; when, reflecting that remaining thus idle, I should not only be very soon out of funds, but should run the risk of being suspected and apprehended as one belonging to one of the numerous gangs of pick-pockets &c. which infest the streets of the city; I applied to an Intelligence Office for a coachman's berth, which I was so fortunate as to procure, at 15 shillings per week—my employer (J. Hyslop, Esq.) although rigid in his exactions, was punctual in his payments, and by my strict prudence and abstinence from the numerous diversions of the city, I was enabled in the six months which I served him, to lay up more cash than what I had earned the twelve months preceding. The next business in which I engaged was that of brick making, and which together with that of gardening, I pursued in the summer seasons almost exclusively for five years; in all which time I was not once suspected of being an American, yet, I must confess that my feelings were not unfrequently most powerfully wrought upon, by hearing my countrymen dubbed with cowardice, and by those too who had been thrice flogged or frightened by them when attempting to ascend the heights of Bunker Hill! and to be obliged to brook these insults with impunity, as to have resented them would have caused me to have been suspected directly of being attached to the American cause, which might have been attended with serious consequences.

I should now pass over the five years that I was employed as above mentioned, as checquered by few incidents worth relating, was it not for one or two circumstances of some little importance that either attended me, or came within my own personal knowledge. The reader has undoubtedly heard that the city of London and its suburbs, is always more or less infested with gangs of nefarious wretches, who come under the denomination of Robbers, Pickpockets, Shoplifters, Swindlers, Beggars, &c. who are constantly prowling the streets in disguise, seeking opportunities to surprise and depredate on the weak and unguarded—of these the former class form no inconsiderable portion, who contrive to elude and set at defiance the utmost vigilance of government—they are a class who in the day time disperse each to his avocation, as the better to blind the scrutinizing eye of justice, they make it a principle to follow some laborious profession, and at night assemble to proceed on their nocturnal rounds, in quest of those whose well stored pockets promise them a reward, equal to the risk which they run in obtaining it. As I was one evening passing through Hyde Park, with five guineas and a few pennies in my pockets, I was stopped by six of these lawless footpads; who, presenting pistols to my breast, demanded my money—fortunately for me I had previously deposited the guineas in a private pocket of my pantaloons, for their better security; thrusting their hands into my other pockets and finding me in possession of but a few English pennies, they took them and decamped. I hastened to Bow Street and lodged information of the robbery with the officers, and who to my no little surprise informed me that mine was the fifth instance, of information of similar robberies by the same gang, which had been lodged with them that evening!—runners had been sent in every direction in pursuit of them, but with what success I could never learn.

Despairing of meeting with a favourable opportunity to return to America, until the conclusion of peace, and the prospects of a continuation of the war being as great then (by what I could learn) as at any period from its commencement, I became more reconciled to my situation, and contracted an intimacy with a young woman whose parents were poor but respectable, and who I soon after married. I took a small ready furnished chamber, in Red Cross Street, where with the fruits of my hard earnings, I was enabled to live tolerable comfortable for three or four years—when, by sickness and other unavoidable circumstances, I was doomed to endure miseries uncommon to human nature.

In the winter of 1781, news was received in London of the surrender of the army of Lord Cornwallis, to the French and American forces!—the receipt of news of an event so unexpected operated on the British ministers and members of Parliament, like a tremendous clap of thunder—deep sorrow was evidently depicted in the countenances of those who had been the most strenuous advocates for the war—never was there a time in which I longed more to exult, and to declare myself a true blooded yankee—and what was still more pleasing to me, was to find myself even surpassed in express-sions of joy and satisfaction, by my wife, in conse-quence of the receipt of news, which, while it went to establish the military fame of my countrymen, was so calculated to humble the pride of her own! greater proofs of her regard for me and my country I could not require.

The ministerial party in Parliament who had been the instigators of the war, and who believed that even a view of the bright glistening muskets and bayonets of John Bull, would frighten the leather apron Yankees to a speedy submission, began now to harbour a more favourable opinion of the courage of the latter. His Majesty repaired immediately to the house of peers, and opened the sessions of parliament—warm debates took place, on account of the ruinous manner in which the American war was continued; but Lord North and his party ap-peared yet unwilling to give up the contest. The capitulation of Cornwallis had however one good effect, as it produced the immediate release of Mr. Laurens from the Tower, and although it did not put an immediate end to the war, yet all hopes of conquering America from that moment appeared to be given up by all except North and his adher-ents.

There was no one engaged in the cause of Ameri-ca, that did more to establish her fame in England, and to satisfy the high boasting Britains of the bravery and unconquerable resolutions of the Yan-

kees, than that bold adventurer capt. Paul Jones;
who, for ten or eleven months kept all the western
coast of the island in alarm—he boldly landed at
Whitehaven, where he burnt a ship in the harbour,
and even attempted to burn the town;—nor was
this to my knowledge the only instance in which
the Britains were threatened with a very serious
conflagration, by the instigation of their enemies
abroad—a daring attempt was made by one James
Aitkin, commonly known in London by the name
of John the Painter, to set fire to the royal dock
and shipping at Portsmouth, and would probably
have succeeded, had he not imprudently communicated his intentions to one, who, for the sake of a
few guineas, shamefully betrayed him—poor Aitkin
was immediately seized, tried, condemned, executed
and hung in chains—every means was used to extort
from him a confession by whom he had been employed, but without any success—it was however
strongly suspected that he had been employed by the
French, as it was about the time that they openly
declared themselves in favour of the Americans.

With regard to Mr. Laurens, I ought to have
mentioned that as soon as I heard of his capture on
his passage to Holland, and of his confinement in
the Tower, I applied for and obtained permission
to visit him in his apartment, and (with some distant hopes that he might point out some way in
which I might be enabled to return to America) I
stated to him every particular as regarded my situ-

ation. He seemed not only to lament very much my hard fortune, but (to use his own words) "that America should be deprived of the services of such men, at the important period too when she most required them."—He informed me that he was himself held a prisoner, and knew not when or on what conditions he would be liberated, but should he thereafter be in a situation to assist me in obtaining a passage to America, he should consider it a duty which he owed his country to do it.

Although I succeeded in obtaining by my industry a tolerable living for myself and family, yet, so far from becoming reconciled to my situation, I was impatient for the return of Peace, when (as I then flattered myself) I should once more have an opportunity to return to my native country. I became every day less attached to a country where I could not meet with any thing (with the exception of my little family) that could compensate me for the loss of the pleasing society of my kindred and friends in America—born among a moral and humane people, and having in my early days contracted their habits, and a considerable number of their prejudices, it would be unnatural to suppose that I should not prefer their society, to either that of rogues, thieves, pimps and vagabonds, or of a more honest but an exceedingly oppressed and forlorn people.

I found London as it had been represented to me, a large and magnificent city, filled with inhabitants of almost every description and occupation—and such an one indeed as might be pleasing to an Englishman, delighting in tumult and confusion, and accustomed to witness scenes of riot and dissipation, as well as those of human infliction; and for the sake of variety, would be willing to imprison himself within the walls of a Bedlam, where continual noise would deafen him, where the unwholesomeness of the air would effect his lungs, and where the closeness of the surrounding buildings would not permit him to enjoy the enlivening influence of the sun! There is not perhaps another city of its size in the whole world, the streets of which display a greater contrast in the wealth and misery, the honesty and knavery, of its inhabitants, than the city of London. The eyes of the passing stranger (unaccustomed to witness such scenes) is at one moment dazzled by the appearance of pompous wealth, with its splendid equippage—at the next he is solicited by one apparently of the most wretched of human beings, to impart a single penny for the relief of his starving family! Among the latter class, there are many; however, who so far from being the real objects of charity that they represent themselves to be, actually possess more wealth than those who sometimes benevolently bestow it—these vile imposters, by every species of deception that was ever devised or practiced by man, aim to excite the pity and compassion, and to extort charity from those unacquainted with their easy circumstances—they possess the faculty of assuming any character that may best suit their purpose—

sometimes hobbling with a crutch and exhibiting a
wooden leg—at other times "an honourable scar of a
wound, received in Egypt, at Waterloo or at Trafalgar, fighting for their most gracious sovereign and
master King George!"

Independent of these there is another species of
beggars (the gypsies) who form a distinct clan, and
will associate with none but those of their own tribe
—they are notorious thieves as well as beggars, and
constantly infest the streets of London to the great
annoyance of strangers and those who have the appearance of being wealthy—they have no particular
home or abiding place, but encamp about in open
fields or under hedges, as occasion requires—they
are generally of a yellow complexion, and converse
in a dialect peculiar only to themselves—their thieving propensities do not unfrequently lead them to
kidnap little children, whenever an opportunity pre-
sents; having first by a dye changed their complexion to one that corresponds with their own, they
represent them as their own offspring, and carry them
about half naked on their backs to excite the pity
and compassion of those of whom they beg charity.
An instance of this species of theft by a party of these
unprincipled vagabonds, occurred once in my neighbourhood while an inhabitant of London—the little
girl kidnapped was the daughter of a Capt. Kellem
of Coventry Street—being sent abroad on some business for her parents, she was met by a gang of Gypsies, consisting of five men and six women, who seized

her, and forcibly carried her away to their camp, in the country, at a considerable distance, having first stripped her of her own cloathes, and in exchange dressed her in some of their rags—thus garbed she travelled about the country with them for nearly 7 months, and was treated as the most abject slave, and her life threatened if she should endeavour to escape or divulged her story;—she stated that during the time she was with them they entrapped a little boy about her own age, whom they also stripped and carried with them, but took particular care he should never converse with her, treating him in the like savage manner; she said that they generally travelled by cross roads and private ways, ever keeping a watchful eye that she might not escape, and that no opportunity offered until when, by some accident, they were obliged to send her from their camp to a neighbouring farm house, in order to procure a light, which she took advantage of; and scrambling over hedges and ditches, as she supposed for the distance of 8 or 9 miles, reached London worn out with fatigue and hunger, her support with them being always scanty, and of the worst sort; to which was added the misery of sleeping under hedges, and exposure to the inclemency of the weather—it was the intention of the gypsies she said to have coloured her and the boy when the walnut season approached.

The streets of London and its suburbs are also infested with another and a still more dreadful species of rogues, denominated Footpads, and who often murder in the most inhuman manner, for the sake of only a few shillings, any unfortunate people who happen to fall in their way—of this I was made acquainted with enumerable instances, while an inhabitant of London; I shall however mention but two that I have now recollection of:—

A Mr. Wylde while passing through Marlborough Street, in a chaise, was stopped by a footpad, who, on demanding his money, received a few shillings, but being dissatisfied with the little booty he obtained, still kept a pistol at Mr. Wylde's head, and on the latter's attempting gently to turn it aside, the villain fired, and lodged seven slugs in his head and breast, which caused instant death—Mr. W. expired in the arms of his son and grandson without a groan. A few days after as a Mr. Greenhill was passing through York-Street in a single horse chaise, he was met and stopped by three footpads, armed with pistols, one of them seized and held the horse's head, while the other two most inhumanely dragged Mr. G. over the back of his chaise, and after robbing him of his notes, watch and hat gave him two severe cuts on his head and left him in that deplorable state in the road.— The above are but two instances of hundreds of a similar nature, which yearly occur in the most public streets of the city of London. The city is infested with a still higher order of rogues, denominated pickpockets or cutpurses, who to carry on their nefarious practices, garb themselves like gentlemen, and introduce themselves into the most fashionable circles;

many of them indeed are persons who once sustained respectable characters, but who, by extravagance and excesses, have reduced themselves to want and find themselves obliged at last to have recourse to pilfering and thieving.

Thus have I endeavoured to furnish the reader with the particulars of a few of the vices peculiar to a large portion of the inhabitants of the city of London —to these might be added a thousand other misdemeanors of a less criminal nature, daily practiced by striplings from the age of six, to the hoary headed of ninety!—this I assure my readers is a picture correctly delineated and not too highly wrought of a city famous for its magnificence, and where I was doomed to spend more than 40 years of my life, and in which time pen, ink, and paper would fail, were I to attempt to record the various instances of misery and want that attended me and my poor devoted family.

In September 1783, the glorious news of a definitive treaty of Peace having been signed between the United States and Great-Britain, was publicly announced in London—while on the minds of those who had been made rich by the war, the unwelcomed news operated apparently like a paralytic stroke, a host of those whose views had been inimical to the cause of America, and had sought refuge in England, attempted to disguise their disappointment and dejection under a veil of assumed cheerfulness. As regarded myself, I can only say, that had an event so long and ardently wished for by me taken place but

a few months before, I should have hailed it as the
epoch of my deliverance from a state of oppression
and privation that I had already too long endured.

An opportunity indeed now presented for me to
return once more to my native country, after so
long an absence, had I possessed the means; but
much was the high price demanded for a passage,
and such had been my low wages, and the expenses
attending the support of even a small family in London, that I found myself at this time in possession
of funds hardly sufficient to defray the expense of
my own passage, and much less that of my wife and
child—hence the only choice left me was either to
desert them, and thereby subject them (far separated from one) to the frowns of an uncharitable
people, or to content myself to remain with them
and partake of a portion of that wretchedness which
even my presence could not avert. When the affairs
of the American Government had become so far
regulated as to support a Consul at the British court,
I might indeed have availed myself individually,
of the opportunity which presented of procuring
a passage home at the Government's expence; but
as this was a privilege that could not be extended
to my wife and child, my regard for them prevented
my embracing the only means provided by my
country for the return of her captured soldiers and
seamen.

To make the best of my hard fortune, I became
as resigned and reconciled to my situation as cir-

cumstances would admit of; flattering myself that
fortune might at some unexpected moment so far
decide in my favour, as to enable me to accomplish
my wishes—I indeed bore my afflictions with a degree of fortitude which I could hardly have believed
myself possessed of—I had become an expert workman at brick making at which business and at
gardening, I continued to work for very small wages,
for three or four years after the Peace—but still
found my prospects of a speedy return to my
country, by no ways flattering. The peace had
thrown thousands who had taken an active part in
the war, out of employ; London was thronged with
them—who, in preference to starving, required no
other consideration for their labour than a humble
living, which had a lamentable effect in reducing
the wages of the labouring class of people; who,
previous to this event were many of them so extremely poor, as to be scarcely able to procure the
necessaries of life for their impoverished families
—among this class I must rank myself, and from
this period ought I to date the commencement of
my greatest miseries, which never failed to attend
me in a greater or less degree until that happy moment, when favoured by providence, I was permitted once more to visit the peaceful shores of the
land of my nativity.

When I first entered the city of London, I was
almost stunned, while my curiosity was not a little
excited by what is termed the "cries of London"

—the streets were thronged by persons of both sexes and of every age, crying each the various articles which they were exposing for sale, or for jobs of work at their various occupations;—I little then thought that this was a mode which I should be obliged myself to adopt to obtain a scanty pittance for my needy family—but, such indeed proved to be the case. The great increase of labourers produced by the cessation of hostilities, had so great an effect in the reduction of wages, that the trifling consideration now allowed me by my employers for my services, in the line of business in which I had been several years engaged, was no longer an object, being insufficient to enable me to procure a humble sustenance. Having in vain sought for more profitable business, I was induced to apply to an acquaintance for instruction in the art of chair bottoming, and which I partially obtained from him for a trifling consideration.

It was now (which was in the year 1789) that I assumed a line of business very different from that in which I had ever before been engaged—fortunately for me, I possessed strong lungs, which I found very necessary in an employment the success of which depended, in a great measure, in being enabled to drown the voices of others (engaged in the same occupation) by my own—"Old Chairs to Mend," became now my constant cry through the streets of London, from morning to night; and although I found my business not so profitable as I could have wished, yet it yielded a tolerable support for my family some time, and probably would have continued so to have done, had not the almost constant illness of my children, rendered the expenses of my family much greater than they otherwise would have been—thus afflicted by additional cares and expense, (although I did every thing in my power to avoid it) I was obliged, to alleviate the sufferings of my family, to contract some trifling debts which it was not in my power to discharge.

I now became the victim of additional miseries—I was visited by a bailiff employed by a creditor, who seizing me with the claws of a tiger, dragged me from my poor afflicted family and inhumanly thurst me into prison! indeed no misery that I ever before endured equalled this—separated from those dependent on me for the necessaries of life, and placed in a situation in which it was impossible for me to afford them any relief!—fortunately for me at this melancholly moment, my wife enjoyed good health, and it was to her praise-worthy exertions that her poor helpless children, as well as myself, owed our preservation from a state of starvation!—this good woman had become acquainted with many who had been my customers, whom she made acquainted with my situation, and the sufferings of my family, and who had the humanity to furnish me with work during my confinement—the chairs were conveyed to and from the prison by my wife—in this way I was enabled to support myself and to contribute something to the relief of my afflicted family. I had in vain represented to my unfeeling creditor my inability to satisfy his demands, and in vain represented to him the suffering condition of those wholly dependent on me; unfortunately for me, he proved to be one of those human beasts, who, having no soul, take pleasure in tormenting that of others, who never feel but in their own misfortunes, and never rejoice but in the afflictions of others—of such beings, so disgraceful to human nature, I assure the reader London contains not an inconsiderable number.

After having for four months languished in a horrid prison, I was liberated therefrom a mere skeleton; the mind afflicted had tortured the body; so much is the one in subjection to the other—I returned sorrowful and dejected to my afflicted family whom I found in very little better condition. We now from necessity took up our abode in an obscure situation near Moorfields; where, by my constant application to business, I succeeded in earning daily a humble pittance for my family, bearly sufficient however to satisfy the cravings of nature; and to add to my afflictions, some one of my family were almost constantly indisposed.

However wretched my situation there were many others at this period, with whom I was particularly acquainted, whose sufferings were greater if possible than my own; and whom want and misery drove to the commission of crimes, that in any other situation they would probably not have been guilty of. Such was the case of the unfortunate Bellamy, who was capitally convicted and executed for a crime which distresses in his family, almost unexampled, had in a moment of despair, compelled him to commit. He was one who had seen better days, was once a commissioned officer in the army, but being unfortunate he was obliged to quit the service to avoid the horrors of a prison, and was thrown on the world, without a single penny or a single friend. The distresses of his family were such, that they were obliged to live for a considerable time deprived of all sustenance except what they could derive from scanty and precarious meals of potatoes and milk—in this situation his unfortunate wife was confined in child bed —lodging in an obscure garret, she was destitute of every species of those conveniences almost indespensable with females in her condition, being herself without clothes, and to procure a covering for her new born infant, all their resources were exhausted. In this situation his wife and children must inevitably have starved, were it not for the loan of five shillings which he walked from London to Blackheath to borrow. At his trial he made a solemn appeal to heaven, as to the truth of every particular as above stated—and that so far from wishing to exaggerate a single fact, he had suppressed many more instances of calamity scarcely to be paralleled—that after the disgrace brought upon himself by this single transaction, life could not be a boon he would be anxious to solicit, but that nature pleaded in his breast for a deserving wife and helpless child —all however was ineffectual, he was condemned and executed pursuant to his sentence.

I have yet one or two more melancholly instances of the effects of famine to record, the first of which happened within a mile of my then miserable habitation—a poor widow woman, who had been left destitute with five small children, and who had been driven to the most awful extremities by hunger, overpowered at length by the pitiful cries of her wretched offspring, for a morsel of bread, in a fit of despair, rushed into the shop of a baker in the neighbourhood, and seizing a loaf of bread bore it off to the relief of her starving family, and while in the act of dividing it among them, the baker (who had pursued her) entered and charged her with the theft—the charge she did not deny, but plead the starving condition of her wretched family in palliation of the crime!—the baker noticing a platter on the table containing a quantity of roasted meat, he pointed to it as a proof that she could not have been driven to such an extremity by hunger—but, his surprise may be better imagined than described, when being requested by the half distracted mother to approach and inspect more closely the contents of the platter, to find it to consist of the remains of a roasted dog! and which she informed him had been her only food, and that of her poor children, for the three preceding days!—the baker struck with so shocking a proof of the poverty and distress of the wretched family, humanely contributed to their relief until they were admitted into the hospital.

I was not personally acquainted with the family, but I well knew one who was, and who communicated to me the following melancholly particulars of its wretched situation; and with which I now present my readers, as another proof of the deplorable situation of the poor in England, after the close of the American war:—The minister of a parish was sent for to attend the funeral of a deceased person in his neighbourhood, being conducted to the apartment which contained the corpse (and which was the only one improved by the wretched family) he found it so low as to be unable to stand upright in it—in a dark corner of the room stood a three legged stool, which supported a coffin of rough boards, and which contained the body of the wretched mother, who had the day previous expired in labour for the want of assistance. The father was sitting on a little stool over a few coals of fire, and endeavouring to keep the infant warm in his bosom; five of his seven children, half naked, were asking their father for a piece of bread, while another about three years old was standing over the corpse of his mother, and crying, as he was wont to do, "take me, take me, mammy!"— "Mammy is asleep," said one of his sisters with tears in her eyes, "mammy is asleep, Johnny, don't cry, the good nurse has gone to beg you some bread and will soon return!"—In a few minutes after,

an old woman, crooked with age, and clothed in
tatters came hobbling into the room, with a two-
penny loaf in her hand, and after heaving a sigh,
calmly set down, and divided the loaf as far as it
would go among the poor half famished children:
and which she observed was the only food they had
tasted for the last 24 hours! By the kind interposition of the worthy divine, a contribution was immediately raised for the relief of this wretched family.

I might add many more melancholly instances of
the extreme poverty and distress of the wretched
poor of London, and with which I was personally
acquainted; but the foregoing it is presumed will be
sufficient to satisfy the poorest class of inhabitants of
America, that, if deprived of the superfluities, so
long as they can obtain the necessaries of life, they
ought not to murmur, but have reason to thank the
Almighty that they were born Americans. That one
half the world knows not how the other half lives,
is a common and just observation;—complaints and
murmurs are frequent I find among those of the inhabitants of this highly favoured country, who are
not only blessed with the liberty and means of procuring for themselves and their families, the necessaries and comforts, but even many of the luxuries of
life!—they complain of poverty, and yet never knew
what it was to be really poor! having never either
experienced or witnessed such scenes of distress and
woe as I have described, they even suppose their
imaginary wants and privations equal to those of
almost any of the human race!

Let those of my countrymen who thus imagine themselves miserable amid plenty, cross the Atlantic and visit the miserable habitations of real and unaffected woe—if their hearts are not destitute of feeling, they will return satisfied to their own peaceful and happy shores, and pour forth the ejaculations of gratitude to that universal parent, who has given them abundance and exempted them from the thousand ills, under the pressure of which a great portion of his children drag the load of life. Permit me to enquire of such unreasonable murmurers, have you compared your situation and circumstances of which you so much complain, with that of those of your fellow creatures, who are unable to earn by their hard labour even a scanty pittance for their starving families? have you compared your situation and circumstances, with that of those who have hardly ever seen the sun, but live confined in lead mines, stone quarries, and coal pits?—before you call yourselves wretched, take a survey of the gaols in Europe, in which wretched beings who have been driven to the commissions of crimes by starvation, or unfortunate and honest debtors (who have been torn from their impoverished families) are doomed to pine.

So far from uttering unreasonable complaints, the hearts of my highly favoured countrymen ought rather to be filled with gratitude to that Being, by whose assistance they have been enabled to avert so many of the miseries of life, so peculiar to a portion of the oppressed of Europe at the present day—and who after groaning themselves for some time under the yoke of foreign tyranny, succeeded in emancipating themselves from slavery and are now blessed with the sweets of liberty, and the undisturbed enjoyment of their natural rights. Britain, imperious Britain, who once boasted the freedom of her government and the invincible power of her arms—now finds herself reduced to the humiliating necessity of receiving lessons of liberty from those whom till late she despised as slaves!—while our own country on the other hand, like a phoenix from her ashes, having emerged from a long, an expensive and bloody war, and established a constitution upon the broad and immovable basis of national equality, now promises to become the permanent residence of peace, liberty, science, and national felicity.—But, to return to the tale of my own sufferings—

While hundreds were daily becoming the wretched victims of hunger and starvation, I was enabled by my industry to obtain a morsel each day for my family; although this morsel, which was to be divided among four, would many times have proved insufficient to have satisfied the hunger of one—I seldom ever failed from morning to night to cry "old chairs to mend," through the principal streets of the city, but many times with very little success— if I obtained four chairs to rebottom in the course of one day, I considered myself fortunate indeed, but instances of such good luck were very rare; it was more frequent that I did not obtain a single one, and after crying the whole day until I made myself hoarse, I was obliged to return to my poor family at night empty handed.

So many at one time engaged in the same business, that had I not resorted to other means my family must inevitably have starved—while crying "old chairs to mend," I collected all the old rags, bits of paper, nails and broken glass which I could find in the streets, and which I deposited in a bag, which I carried with me for that purpose—these produced me a trifle, and that trifle when other resources failed, procured me a morsel of bread, or a few pounds of potatoes, for my poor wife and children—yet I murmured not as the dispensation of the supreme Arbiter of allotments, which had assigned to me so humbled a line of duty; although I could not have believed once, that I should ever have been brought to such a state of humiliating distress, as would have required such means to alleviate it.

In February 1793, War was declared by Great Britain against the republic of France—and although war is a calamity that ought always to be regretted by friends of humanity, as thousands are undoubtedly thereby involved in misery; yet, no event could have happened at that time productive of so much benefit to me, as this—it was the means of draining the country of those who had been once soldiers, and who, thrown out of employ by the peace, demanded a sum so trifling for their services, as to cause a reduction in the wages of the poor labouring class of people, to a sum insufficient to procure the necessaries of life for their families;—this evil was now removed—the old soldiers preferred an employment more in character of themselves, to doing the drudgery of the city—great inducements were held out to them to enlist, and the army was not long retarded in its operations for the want of recruits. My prospects in being enabled to earn something to satisfy the calls of nature, became now more flattering; —the great number that had been employed during the Peace in a business similar to my own, were now reduced to one half, which enabled me to obtain such an extra number of jobs at chair mending that I no longer found it necessary to collect the scrapings of the streets as I had been obliged to do for the many months past. I was now enabled to purchase for my family two or three pounds of fresh meat each week, an article to which (with one or two exceptions) we had been strangers for more than a year—having subsisted principally on potatoes, oat meal bread, and salt fish, and sometimes, but rarely however, were enabled to treat ourselves to a little skim milk.

Had not other afflictions attended me, I should not have had much cause to complain of very extraordinary hardships or privations from this period, until the conclusion of the war in 1817;—my family had increased, and to increase my cares there was scarcely a week passed but that some one of them was seriously indisposed—of ten children of which I was the father, I had the misfortune to bury seven under five years of age, and two more after they had arrived to the age of twenty—my last and only child now living, it pleased the Almighty to spare to me, to administer help and comfort to his poor afflicted parent, and without whose assistance I should (so far from having been enabled once more to visit the land of my nativity) 'ere this have paid the debt of nature in a foreign land, and that too by a death no less horrible than that of starvation!

As my life was unattended with any very extraordinary circumstance (except the one just mentioned) from the commencement of the war, until the re-establishment of monarchy in France, and the cessation of hostilities on the part of Great Britain, in 1817, I shall commence on the narration of my unparalleled sufferings, from the latter period, until that when by the kind interposition of Providence, I was enabled finally to obtain a passage to my native country; and to bid an adieu, and I hope and trust a final one, to that Island, where I had endured a complication of miseries beyond the power of description.

The peace produced similar effects to that of 1783 —thousands were thrown out of employ and the streets of London thronged with soldiers seeking means to earn a humble subsistence. The cry of "Old Chairs to Mend," (and that too at a very reduced price) was reiterated through the streets of London by numbers who but the month before were at Waterloo fighting the battles of their country—which, so seriously effected my business in this line, that to obtain food (and that of the most humble kind) for my family, I was obliged once more to have recourse to the collecting of scraps of rags, paper, glass, and such other articles of however trifling value that I could find in the streets.

It was at this distressing period, that, in consequence of the impossibility of so great a number who had been discharged from the service procuring a livelihood by honest means, that instances of thefts, and daring robberies, increased throughout Great Britain three fold. Bands of highwaymen and robbers hovered about the vicinity of London in numbers which almost defied suppression; many were taken and executed or transported; but this seemed to render the rest only the more desperately bold and cruel, while house-breaking and assassination were daily perpetrated with new arts and outrages in the very capital. Nor were the starving condition of the honest poor, who were to be met with at all times of day and in every street, seeking something to appease their hunger, less remarkable—unable to procure by any means within their power sustenance sufficient to support nature, some actually became the victims of absolute starvation, as the following melancholly instance will show:—a poor man exhausted by want; dropped down in the street—those who were passing unacquainted with the frequency of such melancholly events, at first thought him intoxicated; but after languishing half an hour, he expired. On the following day, an inquest was held on the body, and the verdict of the jury not giving satisfaction to the Coroner, they adjourned to the next day.—In the interim, two respectable surgeons were engaged to open the body, in which not a particle of nutriment was to be found except a little yellow substance, supposed to be grass, or some crude vegetable; which the poor man had swallowed to appease the cravings of nature!—this lamentable proof confirmed the opinion of the jury, that he died for want of the necessaries of life, and gave their verdict accordingly.

Miserable as was the fate of this man and that of many others, mine was but little better, and would ultimately have been the same, had it not been for the assistance afforded me by my only remaining child, a lad but seven years of age. I had now arrived to an advanced age of life, and although possessing an extraordinary constitution for one of my years, yet by my incessant labours to obtain subsistence for my family, I brought on myself a severe fit of sickness, which confined me three weeks to my chamber; in which time my only sustenance was the produce of a few half pennies, which my poor wife and little son had been able to earn each day by, disposing of matches of their own make, and in collecting and disposing of the articles of small value, of which I have before made mention, which were to be found thinly scattered in the streets. In three weeks it was the will of providence so far to restore to me my strength, as to enable me once more to move abroad in search of something to support nature.

The tenement which I at this time rented and which was occupied by my family, was a small and wretched apartment of a garret, and for which I had obligated myself to pay sixpence per day, which was to be paid at the close of every week; and in case of failure (agreeable to the laws or customs of the land) my furniture was liable to be seized. In consequence of my illness, and other misfortunes, I fell six weeks in arrears for rent; and having returned one evening with my wife and son, from the performance of our daily task, my kind readers may judge what my feelings must have been to find our room stripped of every article (of however trifling value) that it contained!— alas, oh heavens! to what a state of wretchedness were we now reduced! if there was any thing wanting to complete our misery, this additional drop to the cup of our afflictions, more than sufficed. Although the real value of all that they had taken from me, or rather robbed me of, would not if publicly disposed of, have produced a sum probably exceeding five dollars; yet it was our all, except the few tattered garments that we had on our backs, and were serviceable and all important to us in our impoverished situation. Not an article of bedding of any kind was left us on which to repose at night, or a chair or stool on which we could rest our wearied limbs! but, as destitute as we were, and naked as they had left our dreary apartment, we had no other abiding place.

With a few half penny's which were jointly our hard earnings of that day, I purchased a peck of coal and a few pounds of potatoes; which while the former furnished us with a little fire, the latter served for the moment to appease our hunger—by a poor family in an adjoining room I was obliged with the loan of a wooden bench, which served as a seat and a table, from which we partook of our homely fare. In this woeful situation, hovering over a few half consumed coals, we spent a sleepless night. The day's dawn brought additional afflictions—my poor wife who had until this period borne her troubles without a sigh or a murmur, and had passed through hardships and sorrows, which nothing but the Supreme Giver of patience and fortitude, and her perfect confidence in him, could have enabled her to sustain; yet so severe and unexpected a stroke as the last, she could not withstand—I found her in the morning gloomy and dejected, and so extremely feeble as to be hardly able to descend the stairs.

We left our miserable habitation in the morning, with hopes that the wretched spectacle that we presented, weak and emaciated as we were, would move some to pity and induce them to impart that relief which our situations so much required—it would however be almost endless to recount the many rebuffs we met with in our attempts to crave assistance. Some few indeed were more merciful, and whatever their opinion might be of the cause of our misery, the distress they saw us in excited their charity, and for their own sakes were induced to contribute a trifle to our wants. We alternately happened among savages and christians, but even the latter, too much influenced by appearances, were very sparing of their bounty.

With the small trifle that had been charitably bestowed on us, we returned at night to our wretched dwelling, which, stripped as it had been, could promise us but little more than a shelter, and where we spent the night very much as the preceding one.— Such was the debilitated state of my poor wife the ensuing morning, produced by excessive hunger and fatigue, as to render it certain, that sinking under the weight of misery, the hand of death in mercy to her, was about to release her from her long and unparalleled sufferings. I should be afraid of exciting too painful sensations in the minds of my readers, were I to attempt to describe my feelings at this moment, and to paint in all their horror, the miseries which afterward attended me; although so numerous had been my afflictions, that it seemed impossible for any new calamity to be capable of augmenting them;—men accustomed to vicissitudes are not soon dejected, but there are trials which human nature alone cannot surmount—indeed to such a state of wretchedness was I now reduced, that had it not been for my suffering family, life would have been

no longer desirable. The attendance that the helpless situation of my poor wife now demanded, it was
not within my power to afford her, as early the next
day I was reluctantly driven by hunger abroad in
search of something that might serve to contribute to
our relief. I left my unfortunate companion, attended by no other person but our little son, destitute of fuel and food, and stretched on an armful of
straw, which I had been so fortunate as to provide
myself with the day preceding;—the whole produce
of my labours this day (which I may safely say was
the most melancholly one of my life) amounted to
no more than one shilling! which I laid out to the
best advantage possible, in the purchase of a few of
the necessaries, which the situation of my sick companion most required.

I ought to have mentioned, that previous to this
melancholy period, when most severely afflicted, I
had been two or three times driven to the necessity
of making application to the Overseers of the poor,
of the parish in which I resided, for admittance into
the Almshouse, or for some assistance, but never
with any success; having always been put off by them
with some evasive answer or frivolous pretence—
sometimes charged by them with being an imposter,
and that laziness more than debility and real want,
had induced me to make the application—at other
times I was told that being an American born, I had
no lawful claim on the government of that country
for support; that I ought to have made application

to the American Consul for assistance, whose business it was to assist such of his countrymen whose situations required it.

But such now was my distress, in consequence of the extreme illness of my wife, that I must receive that aid so indispensably necessary at this important crisis, or subject myself to witness a scene no less distressing, than that of my poor wretched wife, actually perishing for the want of that care and nourishment which it was not in my power to afford her! Thus situated I was induced to renew my application to the Overseer for assistance, representing to him the deplorable situation of my family, who were actually starving for the want of that sustenance which it was not in my power to procure for them; and what I thought would most probably effect his feelings, described to him the peculiar and distressing situation of my wife, the hour of whose dissolution was apparently fast approaching—but, I soon found that I was addressing one who possessed a heart callous to the feelings of humanity—one, whose feelings were not to be touched by a representation of the greatest misery with which human nature could be afflicted. The same cruel observations were made as before, that I was a vile impostor who was seeking by imposition to obtain that support in England, which my own country had withheld from me—that the American Yankees had fought for and obtained their Independence, and yet were not independent enough to support their own poor!—that

Great Britain would find enough to do, was she to afford relief to every d—d yankee vagabond that should apply for it!—fortunately for this abusive British scoundrel, I possessed not now that bodily strength and activity, which I could once boast of, or the villain (whether within his Majesty's dominions or not) should have received on the spot a proof of "Yankee Independence" for his insolence.

Failing in my attempts to obtain the assistance which the lamentable situation of my wife required, I had recourse to other means—I waited on two or three gentlemen in my neighbourhood, who had been represented to me as persons of humanity, and entreated them to visit my wretched dwelling, and to satisfy themselves by occular demonstration, of the state of my wretchedness, especially that of my dying companion—they complied with my request, and were introduced by me to a scene, which for misery and distress, they declared surpassed every thing that they had ever before witnessed!—they accompanied me immediately to one in whom was invested the principal government of the poor of the parish, and represented to him, the scene of human misery which they had been an eye witness to—whereupon an order was issued to have my wife conveyed to the Hospital, which was immediately done and where she was comfortably provided for—but, alas, the relief which her situation had so much required, had been too long deferred—her deprivation and sufferings had been too great to admit of her being now restored to her former state of health, or relieved by any thing that could be administered—after her removal to the Hospital, she lingered a few days in a state of perfect insensibility, and then closed her eyes forever on a world, where for many years, she had been the unhappy subject of almost constant affliction.

I felt very sensibly the irreparable loss of one who had been my companion in adversity, as well as in prosperity; and when blessed with health, had afforded me by her industry that assistance, without which, the sufferings of our poor children would have been greater if possible than what they were. My situation was now truly a lonely one, bereaved of my wife, and all my children except one; who, although but little more than seven years of age, was a child of that sprightliness and activity, as to possess himself with a perfect knowledge of the chair-bottoming business, and by which he earned not only enough (when work could be obtained) to furnish himself with food, but contributed much to the relief of his surviving parent, when confined by illness and infirmity.

We continued to improve the apartment from which my wife had been removed, until I was so fortunate as to be able to rent a ready furnished apartment (as it was termed) at four shillings and sixpence per week. Apartments of this kind are not uncommon in London, and are intended to accommodate poor families, situated as we were, who had been so unfortunate as to be stripped of every thing but the cloathes on their backs by their unfeeling landlords. These "ready furnished rooms" were nothing but miserable apartments in garrets, and contain but few more conveniences than what many of our common prisons in America afford—a bunk of straw, with two or three old blankets, a couple of chairs, and a rough table about three feet square, with an article or two of iron ware in which to cook our victuals (if we should be so fortunate as to obtain any) was the contents of the "ready furnished apartment" that we were now about to occupy—but even with these few conveniences, it was comparatively a palace to the one we had for several weeks past improved.

When my health would permit, I seldom failed to visit daily the most public streets of the city, and from morning to night cry for old chairs to mend—accompanied by my son Thomas, with a bundle of flags, as represented in the Plate annexed to this volume. If we were so fortunate as to obtain a job of work more than we could complete in the day, with the permission of the owner, I would convey the chairs on my back to my humble dwelling, and with the assistance of my little son, improve the evening to complete the work, which would produce us a few half pennies to purchase something for our breakfast the next morning—but it was very seldom that instances of this kind occurred, as it was more frequently the case that after crying for old chairs to mend, the whole day, we were obliged to return, hungry and

weary, and without a single half penny in our pockets,
to our humble dwelling, where we were obliged to
fast until the succeeding day; and indeed there were
some instances in which we were compelled to fast
two or three days successively, without being able
to procure a single job of work.—The rent I had
obligated myself to pay every night, and frequently
when our hunger was such as hardly to be endured,
I was obliged to reserve the few pennies that I was
possessed of to apply to this purpose.

In our most starving condition when every other
plan failed, my little son would adopt the expedient
of sweeping the public cause-ways (leading from one
walk to the other) where he would labour the whole
day, with the expectation of receiving no other reward than what the generosity of gentlemen, who
had occasion to cross, would induce them to bestow
in charity, and which seldom amounted to more
than a few pennies—sometime the poor boy would
toil in this way the whole day, without being so
fortunate as to receive a single half penny—it was
then he would return home sorrowful and dejected,
and while he attempted to conceal his own hunger,
with tears in his eyes, would lament his hard fortune
in not being able to obtain something to appease
mine.—While he was thus employed I remained at
home, but not idle, being as busily engaged in making matches, with which (when he returned home
empty handed) we were obliged as fatigued as we
were, to visit the markets to expose for sale, and

where we were obliged sometimes to tarry until eleven o'clock at night, before we could meet with a single purchaser.

Having one stormy night of a Saturday, visited the market with my son for this purpose, and after exposing ourselves to the chilling rain until past 10 o'clock, without being able either of us to sell a single match, I advised the youth (being thinly clad) to return home feeling disposed to tarry myself a while longer, in hopes that better success might attend me, as having already fasted one day and night, it was indispensably necessary that I should obtain something to appease our hunger the succeeding day (Sunday) or what seemed almost impossible, to endure longer its torments! I remained until the clock struck eleven, the hour at which the market closed, and yet had met with no better success! It is impossible to describe the sensation of despondency which overwhelmed me at this moment! I now considered it as certain that I must return home with nothing wherewith to satisfy our craving appetites —and with my mind filled with the most heart rending reflections, I was about to return, when, Heaven seemed pleased to interpose in my behalf, and to send relief when I little expected it;—passing a beef stall I attracted the notice of the butcher, who viewing me, probably as I was, a miserable object of pity, emaciated by long fastings, and clad in tattered garments, from which the water was fast dripping, and judging no doubt by my appearance that on no one could charity be more properly bestowed, he threw into my basket a beeve's heart, with the request that I would depart with it immediately for my home, if any I had!—I will not attempt to describe the joy that I felt on this occasion, in so unexpectedly meeting with that relief, which my situation so much required. I hastened home with a much lighter heart than what I had anticipated; and when I arrived, the sensations of joy exhibited by my little son on viewing the prize that I bore, produced effects as various as extraordinary; he wept, then laughed and danced with transport.

The reader must suppose that while I found it so extremely difficult to earn enough to preserve us from starvation, I had little to spare for cloathing and other necessaries; and that this was really my situation, I think no one will doubt, when I positively declare that to such extremities was I driven, that being unable to pay a barber for shaving me, I was obliged to adopt the expedient for more than two years, of clipping my beard as close as possible with a pair of scissors which I kept expressly for that purpose!—as strange and laughable as the circumstance may appear to some, I assure the reader that I state facts, and exaggerate nothing. As regarded our cloathes, I can say no more than that they were the best that we could procure, and were such as persons in our situations were obliged to wear—they served to conceal our nakedness, but would have proved insufficient to have protected our bodies, from the inclemency of the weather of a colder climate. Such indeed was sometimes our miserable appearance, clad in tattered garments, that while engaged in our employment in crying for old chairs to mend, we not only attracted the notice of many, but there were instances in which a few half pennies unsolicited were bestowed on us in charity—an instance of this kind happened one day as I was passing through threadneedle street; a gentleman perceiving by the appearance of the shoes that I wore, that they were about to quit me, put a half crown in my hand, and bid me go and cry "old shoes to mend!"

In long and gloomy winter evenings, when unable to furnish myself with any other light than that emitted by a little fire of sea coal, I would attempt to drive away melancholy by amusing my son with an account of my native country, and of the many blessings there enjoyed by even the poorest class of people—of their fair fields producing a regular supply of bread—their convenient houses, to which they could repair after the toils of the day, to partake of the fruits of their labour, safe from the storms and the cold, and where they could lay down their heads to rest without any to molest them or to make them afraid. Nothing could have been better calculated to excite animation in the mind of the poor child, than an account so flattering of a country which had given birth to his father, and to which he had received my repeated assurances he should accompany me as soon as an opportunity should present—after expressing his fears that the happy day was yet far distant, with a deep sigh he would exclaim "would to God it was to morrow!"

About a year after the decease of my wife, I was taken extremely ill, insomuch that at one time my life was dispaired of, and had it not been for the friendless and lonely situation in which such an event would have placed my son, I should have welcomed the hour of my dissolution and viewed it as a consummation rather to be wished than dreaded; for so great had been my sufferings of mind and body, and the miseries to which I was still exposed, that life had really become a burden to me—indeed I think it would have been difficult to have found on the face of the earth a being more wretched than I had been for the three years past.

During my illness my only friend on earth was my son Thomas, who did every thing to alleviate my wants within the power of his age to do—sometimes by crying for old chairs to mend (for he had become as expert a workman at this business as his father) and sometimes by sweeping the cause-ways, and by making and selling matches, he succeeded in earning each day a trifle sufficient to procure for me and himself a humble sustenance. When I had so far recovered as to be able to creep abroad, and the youth had been so fortunate as to obtain a good job, I would accompany him, although very feeble, and assist him in conveying the chairs home—it was on such occasions that my dear child would manifest his tenderness and affection for me, by insisting (if there were four chairs) that I should carry but one, and he would carry the remaining three, or in that proportion if a greater or less number.

From the moment that I had informed him of the many blessings enjoyed by my countrymen of every class, I was almost constantly urged by my son to apply to the American Consul for a passage—it was in vain that I represented to him, that if such an application was attended with success and the opportunity should be improved by me, it must cause our separation, perhaps forever; as he would not be permitted to accompany me at the expense of government—"never mind me (he would reply) do not father suffer any more on my account; if you can only succeed in obtaining a passage to a country where you can enjoy the blessings that you have described to me, I may hereafter be so fortunate as to meet with an opportunity to join you—and if not, it will be a consolation to me, whatever my afflictions may be, to think that yours have ceased!" My ardent wish to return to America, was not less than that of my son, but could not bear the thoughts of a separation; of leaving him behind exposed to all the miseries peculiar to the friendless poor of that country;—he was a child of my old age, and from whom I had received too many proofs of his love and regard for me, not to feel that parental affection for him to which his amiable disposition entitled him.

I was indeed unacquainted with the place of resi-

dence of the American Consul—I had made frequent
enquiries, but found no one that could inform me
correctly where he might be found; but so anxious
was my son that I should spend the remnant of my
days in that country where I should receive (if
nothing more) a christian burial at my decease, and
bid adieu forever to a land where I had spent so
great a portion of my life in sorrow, and many years
had endured the lingering tortures of protracted
famine; that he ceased not to enquire of everyone
with whom he was acquainted, until he obtained the
wished for information. Having learned the place
of residence of the American Consul, and fearful of
the consequences of delay, he would give me no
peace until I promised that I would accompany him
there the succeeding day, if my strength would admit of it; for although I had partially recovered from
a severe fit of sickness, yet I was still so weak and
feeble as to be scarcely able to walk.

My son did not forget to remind me early the next
morning of my promise, and to gratify him more
than with an expectation of meeting with much success I set out with him, feeble as I was, for the Consul's. The distance was about two miles, and before
I had succeeded in reaching half the way, I had
wished myself a dozen times safe home again, and
had it not been for the strong persuasions of my son
to the contrary, I certainly should have returned.—I
was never before so sensible of the effects of my long
sufferings—which had produced that degree of bodily

weakness and debility, as to leave me scarcely strength sufficient to move without the assistance of my son; who, when he found me reeling or halting through weakness, would support me until I had gained sufficient strength to proceed.

Although the distance was but two miles, yet such was the state of my weakness, that although we started early in the morning, it was half past 3 o'-clock P.M. when we reached the Consul's office, when I was so much exhausted as to be obliged to ascend the steps on my hands and knees. Fortunately we found the Consul in, and on my addressing him and acquainting him with the object of my visit, he seemed at first unwilling to credit the fact that I was an American born—but after interrogating me some-time, as to the place of my nativity, the cause which first brought me to England, &c. he seemed to be more satisfied; he however observed (on being in-formed that the lad who accompanied me was my son) that he could procure a passage for me, but not for him, as being born in England, the American government would consider him a British subject, and under no obligation to defray the expence of his passage—and as regarded myself, he observed, that he had his doubts, so aged and infirm as I appeared to be, whether I should live to reach America, if I should attempt it.

I cannot say that I was much surprised at the observations of the Consul, as they exactly agreed with what I had anticipated—and as anxious as I then

felt to visit once more my native country, I felt determined not to attempt it, unless I could be accompanied by my son, and expressed myself to this effect
to the Consul—the poor lad appeared nearly over-
come with grief when he saw me preparing to return
without being able to effect my object; indeed so
greatly was he affected, and such the sorrow that he
exhibited, that he attracted the notice (and I believe
I may add the pity) of the Consul—who, after making some few enquiries as regarded his disposition,
age, &c. observed that he could furnish the lad with
a passage at his own expense, which he should have
no objection to do if I would consent to his living
with a connection of his (the Consul.) on his arrival
in America—"but (continued he,) in such a case you
must be a while separated, for it would be imprudent
for you to attempt the passage until you have gained
more strength—I will pay your board, where by better
living than you have been latterly accustomed to,
you may have a chance to recruit—but your son must
take passage on board the London Packet, which sails
for Boston the day after to-morrow."

Although but a few moments previous, my son
would have thought no sacrifice too great, that would
have enabled us to effect our object in obtaining passages to America; yet, when he found that instead of
himself, I was to be left for a while behind, he appeared at some loss how to determine—but on being
assured by the Consul that if my life was spared I
should soon join him, he consented; and being fur-

nished by the Consul with a few necessary articles of cloathing, I the next day accompanied him on board the packet which was to convey him to America— and after giving him the best advice that I was capable of as regarded his behaviour and deportment while on his passage, and on his arrival in America, I took my leave of him and saw him not again until I met him on the wharf on my arrival at Boston.

When I parted with the Consul he presented me with half a crown, and directions where to apply for board—it was at a public Inn where I found many American seamen, who, like myself, were boarded there at the Consul's expence, until passages could be obtained for them to America—I was treated by them with much civility, and by hearing them daily recount their various and remarkable adventures, as well as by relating my own, I passed my time more agreeably than what I probably should have done in other society.

In eight weeks I was so far recruited by good living, as in the opinion of the Consul, to be able to endure the fatigues of a passage to my native country, and which was procured for me on board the ship Carterian, bound to New-York. We set sail on the 5th April, 1823, and after a passage of 42 days, arrived safe at our port of destination. After having experienced in a foreign land so much ill-treatment from those from whom I could expect no mercy, and for no other fault than that of being an American, I could not but flatter myself that when I bid adieu to that country, I should no longer be the subject of unjust persecution, or have occasion to complain of ill treatment from those whose duty it was to afford me protection. But the sad reverse which I experienced while on board the Carterian, convinced me of the incorrectness of my conclusions. For my country's sake, I am happy that I have it in my power to say that the crew of this ship, was not composed altogether of Americans—there was a mixture of all nations; and among them some so vile, and destitute of every humane principle, as to delight in nothing so much as to sport with the infirmities of one, whose grey locks ought at least to have protected him. By these unfeeling wretches (who deserve not the name of sailors) I was not only most shamefully ill-used on the passage, but was robbed of some necessary articles of cloathing, which had been charitably bestowed on me by the American Consul.

We arrived in the harbour of New-York about midnight, and such were the pleasing sensations produced by the reflection that on the morrow I should be indulged with the priviledge of walking once more on American ground after an absence of almost 50 years, and that but a short distance now separated me from my dear son, that it was in vain that I attempted to close my eyes to sleep. Never was the morning's dawn so cheerfully welcomed by me. I solicited and obtained the permission of the captain to be early set on shore, and on reaching which, I did not forget to offer up my unfeigned thanks to that Almighty Being, who had not only sustained me during my heavy afflictions abroad, but had finally restored me to my native country. The pleasure that I enjoyed in viewing the streets thronged by those, who, although I could not claim as acquaintances, I could greet as my countrymen, was unbounded, I felt a regard for almost every object that met my eyes, because it was American.

Great as was my joy on finding myself once more among my countrymen, I felt not a little impatient for the arrival of the happy moment when I should be able to meet my son. Agreeable to the orders which I received from the American Consul, I applied to the Custom House in New-York for a passage from thence to Boston, and with which I was provided on board a regular packet which sailed the morning ensuing—in justice to the captain, I must say that I was treated by him as well as by all on board, with much civility. We arrived at the Long Wharf in Boston after a short and pleasant passage. I had been informed by the Consul, previous to leaving London, of the name of the gentleman with whom my son probably lived, and a fellow passenger on board the packet was so good as to call on and inform him of my arrival—in less than fifteen minutes after receiving the information my son met me on the wharf! Reader, you will not believe it possible for me to describe my feelings correctly at this joyful moment! if you are a parent, you may have some conception of them; but a faint one however unless you and an only and beloved child have been placed in a similar situation.

After acquainting myself with the state of my boy's health, &c. my next enquiry was whether he found the country as it had been described by me, and how he esteemed it—"well, extremely well (was his reply) since my arrival I have fared like a Prince, I have meat every day, and have feasted on American puddings and pies (such as you used to tell me about) until I have become almost sick of them!" I was immediately conducted by him to the house of the gentleman with whom he lived, and by whom I was treated with much hospitality—in the afternoon of the day succeeding (by the earnest request of my son) I visited Bunker Hill, which he had a curiosity to view, having heard it so frequently spoken of by me while in London, as the place where the memorable battle was fought and in which I received my wounds.

I continued in Boston about a fortnight, and then set out on foot to visit once more my native State. My son accompanied me as far as Roxbury, when I was obliged reluctantly to part with him, and proceeded myself no farther on my journey that day than Jamaica plains, where at a public house I tarried all night—from thence I started early the next morning and reached Providence about 5 o'clock in the afternoon, and obtained lodgings at a public Inn in High-Street.

It may not be improper here to acquaint my readers that as I had left my father possessed of very considerable property, and of which at his decease I thought myself entitled to a portion equal to that of other children, which (as my father was very economical in the management of his affairs) I knew could not amount to a very inconsiderable sum, it was to obtain this if possible, that I became extremely anxious to visit immediately the place of my nativity—accordingly the day after I arrived in Providence, I hastened to Cranston, to seek my connexions if any were to be found; and if not to seek among the most aged of the inhabitants, some one who had not forgotten me, and who might be able to furnish me with the sought for information. But, alas, too soon were blasted my hopeful expectations of finding something in reserve for me, that might have afforded me a humble support, the few remaining years of my life. It was by a distant connection that I was informed that my brothers had many years since removed to a distant part of the country —that having credited a rumour in circulation of my death, at the decease of my father had disposed of the real estate of which he died possessed, and had divided the proceeds equally among themselves! This was another instance of adverse fortune that I had not anticipated!—it was indeed a circumstance so foreign from my mind that I felt myself for the first time, unhappy, since my return to my native country, and even believed myself now doomed to endure, among my own countrymen (for whose liberties I had fought and bled) miseries similar to those that had attended me for many years in Europe. With these gloomy forebodings I returned to Providence, and contracted for board with the gentleman at whose house I had lodged the first night of my arrival in town, and to whom for the kind treatment that I have received from him and his family, I shall feel till death under the deepest obligations that gratitude can dictate; for I can truly say of him, that I was a stranger and he took me in, I was hungry and naked, and he fed and cloathed me.

As I had never received any remuneration for services rendered, and hardships endured in the cause of my country, I was now obliged, as my last resort, to petition Congress to be included in that number of the few surviving soldiers of the Revolution, for whose services they had been pleased to grant pensions—and I would to God that I could add, for the honour of my country, that the application met with its deserving success—but, although accompanied by the deposition of a respectable gentleman (which deposition I have thought proper to annex to my narrative) satisfactorily confirming every fact as therein stated—yet, on no other principle, than that *I was absent from the country when the pension law passed*—my Petition was REJECTED!!! Reader, I have been for 30 years (as you will perceive by what I have stated in the foregoing pages) subject, in a *foreign* country, to almost all the miseries with which poor human nature is capable of being inflicted—

yet, in no one instance did I ever feel so great degree of a depression of spirits, as when the fate of my Petition was announced to me! I love too well the country which gave me birth, and entertain too high a respect for those employed in its government, to reproach them with ingratitude; yet, it is my sincere prayer that this strange and unprecedented circumstance, of withholding from me that reward which they have so generally bestowed on others, may never be told in Europe, or published in the streets of London, least it reach the ears of some who had the effrontery to declare to me personally, that for the active part that I had taken in the "rebellious war" misery and starvation would ultimately be my reward!

To conclude—although I may be again unfortunate in a renewal of my application to government, for that reward to which my services so justly entitle me—yet I feel thankful that I am priviledged (after enduring so much) to spend the remainder of my days, among those who I am confident are possessed of too much humanity, to see me suffer; and which I am sensible I owe to the divine goodness, which graciously condescended to support me under my numerous afflictions, and finally enabled me to return to my native country in the 79th year of my age—for this I return unfeigned thanks to the Almighty; and hope to give during the remainder of my life, convincing testimonies of the strong impression which those afflictions made on my mind, by devoting myself sincerely to the duties of religion.

DEPOSITION OF JOHN VIAL

I JOHN VIAL of North Providence, in the county
of Providence, in the State of Rhode Island, on oath
certify and say, that sometime in the latter part of
November or the beginning of December A.D. 1775,
I entered as gunner's mate on board the Washington,
a public armed vessel in the service of the United
States, and under the command of S. Martindale,
Esq.—said vessel was sent out by order of General
WASHINGTON, from Plymouth (Mass.) to cruise in
Boston harbour to intercept supplies going to Boston, then in the possession of the British troops.
After we had been out a short time, we were captured by a British 20 gun ship, called the "Foy,"
and were carried to Boston, where we remained
about a week and were then put on board the
frigate Tartar, and sent to England as prisoners—
and I the said John further testify and say, that I
well remember Israel R. Potter, now residing in
Cranston, who was a mariner on board the Washington also—said Potter entered about the time I
did and was captured and carried to England with
me. We arrived in England in January 1776, we
were then put into the Hospital, the greater part
of the crew being sick in consequence of the confinement during the voyage, where many died—I remained in imprisonment about sixteen months when
I made my escape—what became of said Potter after-

wards I do not know but I have not the least doubt he remained a prisoner until the peace 1783 as he stated in his application for a pension—I have no doubt he suffered a great deal during his captivity. According to my best recollection nearly one third of the crew died in the hospital—I do remember an affair which took place during our voyage to England which caused Potter to suffer a great deal more than perhaps he otherwise would—a number of the crew of the Washington formed a plan to rise and take the Frigate but was defeated in their purpose, among whom I believe Potter was one, and in consequence, put in irons for the remaining part of the voyage with a number of others. And I the said John do further testify that I do not know of any of the said crew of the Washington now being alive except said Potter and myself—and that I do not believe it to be in the power of said Potter to procure any other testimony of the above mentioned facts except mine.

JOHN VIAL.

Rhode Island District—Providence Aug. 6, 1823.

The said John Vial, who is well known to me and is a creditable witness, made solemn oath to the truth of the foregoing deposition by him subscribed in my presence.

DAVID HOWELL.
DISTRICT JUDGE.

APPENDIX

Herman Melville first conceived of retelling the tale of Israel Potter, the "Revolutionary beggar," in 1849 after coming upon a tattered copy of the original book. When he finally wrote his own account in 1854, he drew as well on the narratives of Ethan Allen and Nathaniel Fanning, who had served under John Paul Jones, and he had himself visited London.

While the real Israel Potter devoted half of his personal history to his years in London following the Revolutionary War, Melville retold these events in a few brief concluding chapters to his own volume, *Israel Potter, His Fifty Years of Exile*. Melville's chapters are reproduced from the 1855 first edition to give a comparative view of the tragedy of Potter's life as seen by himself and by Herman Melville, a quarter of a century later.

ISRAEL POTTER:

His Fifty Years of Exile.

BY

HERMAN MELVILLE,

AUTHOR OF "TYPEE," "OMOO," ETC.

New York:
G. P. PUTNAM & CO., 10 PARK PLACE.
1855.

BIOGRAPHY, in its purer form, confined to the ended lives of the true and brave, may be held the fairest meed of human virtue—one given and received in entire disinterestedness—since neither can the biographer hope for acknowledgment from the subject, nor the subject at all avail himself of the biographical distinction conferred.

Israel Potter well merits the present tribute—a private of Bunker Hill, who for his faithful services was years ago promoted to a still deeper privacy under the ground, with a posthumous pension, in default of any during life, annually paid him by the spring in ever-new mosses and sward.

I am the more encouraged to lay this performance at the feet of your Highness, because, with a change in the grammatical person, it preserves, almost as in a reprint, Israel Potter's autobiographical story. Shortly after his return in infirm old age to his native land, a little narrative of his adventures, forlornly published on sleazy gray paper, appeared among the peddlers, written, probably, not by himself, but taken down from his lips by another. But like the crutch-marks of the cripple by the Beautiful Gate, this blurred record is now out of print. From a tattered copy, rescued by the merest chance from the rag-pickers, the present account has been drawn, which, with the exception of some expansions, and additions of historic and personal details, and one or two shiftings of scene, may, perhaps, be not unfitly regarded something in the light of a dilapidated old tombstone retouched.

Well aware that in your Highness' eyes the merit of the story must be in its general fidelity to the main drift of the original narrative, I forbore anywhere to mitigate the hard fortunes of my hero; and particularly towards the end, though sorely tempted, durst not substitute for the allotment of Providence any artistic recompense of poetical justice; so that no one can complain of the gloom of my closing chapters more profoundly than myself.

Such is the work, and such the man, that I have the honor to present to your Highness. That the name here noted should not have appeared in the volumes of Sparks, may or may not be a matter for astonishment ; but Israel Potter seems purposely to have waited to make his popular advent under the present exalted patronage, seeing that your Highness, according to the definition above, may, in the loftiest sense, be deemed the Great Biographer : the national commemorator of such of the anonymous privates of June 17, 1775, who may never have received other requital than the solid reward of your granite.

Your Highness will pardon me, if, with the warmest ascriptions on this auspicious occasion, I take the liberty to mingle my hearty congratulations on the recurrence of the anniversary day we celebrate, wishing your Highness (though indeed your Highness be somewhat prematurely gray) many returns of the same, and that each of its summer's suns may shine as brightly on your brow as each winter snow shall lightly rest on the grave of Israel Potter.

Your Highness'

Most devoted and obsequious,

THE EDITOR.

June 17th, 1854.

CHAPTER XXVI.

FORTY-FIVE YEARS.

FOR the most part, what befell Israel during his forty
years wanderings in the London deserts, surpassed
the forty years in the natural wilderness of the outcast
Hebrews under Moses.

In that London fog, went before him the ever-present
cloud by day, but no pillar of fire by the night, except
the cold column of the monument, two hundred feet
beneath the mocking gilt flames on whose top, at the
stone base, the shiverer, of midnight, often laid down.

But these experiences, both from their intensity and
his solitude, were necessarily squalid. Best not enlarge
upon them. For just as extreme suffering, without hope,
is intolerable to the victim, so, to others, is its depiction
without some corresponding delusive mitigation. The
gloomiest and truthfulest dramatist seldom chooses for
his theme the calamities, however extraordinary, of inferior and private persons; least of all, the pauper's;
admonished by the fact, that to the craped palace of the
king lying in state, thousands of starers shall throng; but

few feel enticed to the shanty, where, like a pealed knuckle-bone, grins the unupholstered corpse of the beggar.

Why at one given stone in the flagging does man after man cross yonder street? What plebeian Lear or Œdipus, what Israel Potter, cowers there by the corner they shun? From this turning point, then, we too cross over and skim events to the end; omitting the particulars of the starveling's wrangling with rats for prizes in the sewers; or his crawling into an abandoned doorless house in St. Giles', where his hosts were three dead men, one pendant; into another of an alley nigh Houndsditch, where the crazy hovel, in phosphoric rottenness, fell sparkling on him one pitchy midnight, and he received that injury, which, excluding activity for no small part of the future, was an added cause of his prolongation of exile, besides not leaving his faculties unaffected by the concussion of one of the rafters on his brain.

But these were some of the incidents not belonging to the beginning of his career. On the contrary, a sort of humble prosperity attended him for a time; insomuch that once he was not without hopes of being able to buy his homeward passage so soon as the war should end. But, as stubborn fate would have it, being run over one day at Holborn Bars, and taken into a neighboring bakery, he was there treated with such kindliness by a Kentish lass, the shop-girl, that in the end he thought his debt of gratitude could only be repaid by love. In a word, the money saved up for his ocean voyage was lavished upon a rash embarkation in wedlock.

Originally he had fled to the capital to avoid the

dilemma of impressment or imprisonment. In the absence of other motives, the dread of those hardships
would have fixed him there till the peace. But now,
when hostilities were no more, so was his money. Some
period elapsed ere the affairs of the two governments
were put on such a footing as to support an American
consul at London. Yet, when this came to pass, he could
only embrace the facilities for a return here furnished,
by deserting a wife and child, wedded and born in the
enemy's land.

The peace immediately filled England, and more especially London, with hordes of disbanded soldiers; thousands of whom, rather than starve, or turn highwaymen
(which no few of their comrades did, stopping coaches at
times in the most public streets), would work for such
a pittance as to bring down the wages of all the laboring
classes. Neither was our adventurer the least among the
sufferers. Driven out of his previous employ—a sort of
porter in a river-side warehouse—by this sudden influx
of rivals, destitute, honest men like himself, with the in-
genuity of his race, he turned his hand to the village art
of chair-bottoming. An itinerant, he paraded the streets
with the cry of "Old chairs to mend!" furnishing a
curious illustration of the contradictions of human life;
that he who did little but trudge, should be giving cosy
seats to all the rest of the world. Meantime, according
to another well-known Malthusian enigma in human affairs,
his family increased. In all, eleven children were born
to him in certain sixpenny garrets in Moorfields. One
after the other, ten were buried.

When chair-bottoming would fail, resort was had to match-making. That business being overdone in turn, next came the cutting of old rags, bits of paper, nails, and broken glass. Nor was this the last step. From the gutter he slid to the sewer. The slope was smooth. In poverty,

——" Facilis descensus Averni."

But many a poor soldier had sloped down there into the boggy canal of Avernus before him. Nay, he had three corporals and a sergeant for company.

But his lot was relieved by two strange things, presently to appear. In 1793 war again broke out, the great French war. This lighted London of some of its superfluous hordes, and lost Israel the subterranean society of his friends, the corporals and sergeant, with whom wandering forlorn through the black kingdoms of mud, he used to spin yarns about sea prisoners in hulks, and listen to stories of the Black Hole of Calcutta; and often would meet other pairs of poor soldiers, perfect strangers, at the more public corners and intersections of sewers—the Charing-Crosses below; one soldier having the other by his remainder button, earnestly discussing the sad prospects of a rise in bread, or the tide; while through the grating of the gutters overhead, the rusty skylights of the realm, came the hoarse rumblings of bakers' carts, with splashes of the flood whereby these unsuspected gnomes of the city lived.

Encouraged by the exodus of the lost tribes of soldiers, Israel returned to chair-bottoming. And it was in frequenting Covent-Garden market, at early morning, for the purchase of his flags, that he experienced one of the strange alleviations hinted of above. That chatting with the ruddy, aproned, hucksterwomen, on whose moist cheeks yet trickled the dew of the dawn on the meadows; that being surrounded by bales of hay, as the raker by cocks and ricks in the field; those glimpses of garden produce, the blood-beets, with the damp earth still tufting the roots; that mere handling of his flags, and bethinking him of whence they must have come, the green hedges through which the wagon that brought them had passed; that trudging home with them as a gleaner with his sheaf of wheat;—all this was inexpressibly grateful. In want and bitterness, pent in, perforce, between dingy walls, he had rural returns of his boyhood's sweeter days among them; and the hardest stones of his solitary heart (made hard by bare endurance alone) would feel the stir of tender but quenchless memories, like the grass of deserted flagging, upsprouting through its closest seams. Sometimes, when incited by some little incident, however trivial in itself, thoughts of home would—either by gradually working and working upon him, or else by an impetuous rush of recollection—overpower him for a time to a sort of hallucination.

Thus was it:—One fair half-day in the July of 1800, by good luck, he was employed, partly out of charity, by one of the keepers, to trim the sward in an oval enclosure within St. James' Park, a little green but a three-minutes' walk along the gravelled way from the brick-besmoked and grimy Old Brewery of the palace which gives its ancient name to the public resort on whose borders it stands. It was a little oval, fenced in with iron pailings, between whose bars the imprisoned verdure peered forth, as some wild captive creature of the woods from its cage. And alien Israel there—at times staring dreamily about him—seemed like some amazed runaway steer, or trespassing Pequod Indian, impounded on the shores of Narraganset Bay, long ago; and back to New England our exile was called in his soul. For still working, and thinking of home; and thinking of home, and working amid the verdant quietude of this little oasis, one rapt thought begat another, till at last his mind settled intensely, and yet half humorously, upon the image of Old Huckleberry, his mother's favorite old pillion horse; and, ere long, hearing a sudden scraping noise (some hob-shoe without, against the iron pailing), he insanely took it to be Old Huckleberry in his stall, hailing him (Israel) with his shod fore-foot clattering against the planks—his customary trick when hungry—and so, down goes Israel's hook, and with a tuft of white clover, impulsively snatched, he hurries away a few paces in obedience to the imaginary summons. But soon stopping midway, and forlornly gazing round at the enclosure, he bethought him that a far different oval, the great oval of the ocean, must be crossed ere his crazy errand could be done; and even then, Old Huckleberry would be found long surfeited with clover, since, doubtless, being dead many a summer, he must be buried beneath it. And many years after, in a far different part of the town, and in far less winsome weather too, passing with his bundle of flags through Red-Cross street, towards Barbican, in a fog so dense that the dimmed and massed blocks of houses, exaggerated by the loom, seemed shadowy ranges on ranges of midnight hills, he heard a confused pastoral sort of sounds—tramplings, lowings, halloos—and was suddenly called to by a voice to head off certain cattle, bound to Smithfield, bewildered and unruly in the fog. Next instant he saw the white face—white as an orange-blossom—of a black-bodied steer, in advance of the drove, gleaming ghost-like through the vapors; and presently, forgetting his limp, with rapid shout and gesture, he was more eager, even than the troubled farmers, their owners, in driving the riotous cattle back into Barbican. Mono-maniac reminiscences were in him—"To the right, to the right!" he shouted, as, arrived at the street corner, the farmers beat the drove to the left, towards Smith-field: "To the right! you are driving them back to the pastures—to the right! that way lies the barn-yard!" "Barn-yard?" cried a voice; "you are dreaming, old man." And so, Israel, now an old man, was bewitched by the mirage of vapors; he had dreamed himself home into the mists of the Housatonic mountains; ruddy boy on the upland pastures again. But how different the flat, apathetic, dead, London fog now seemed from those agile mists which, goat-like, climbed the purple peaks, or in routed armies of phantoms, broke down, pell-mell, dispersed in flight upon the plain, leaving the cattle-boy loftily alone, clear-cut as a balloon against the sky.

In 1817 he once more endured extremity; this second peace again drifting its discharged soldiers on London, so that all kinds of labor were overstocked. Beggars, too, lighted on the walks like locusts. Timber-toed cripples stilted along, numerous as French peasants in *sabots*. And, as thirty years before, on all sides, the exile had heard the supplicatory cry, not addressed to him, "An honorable scar, your honor, received at Bunker Hill, or Saratoga, or Trenton, fighting for his most gracious Majesty, King George!" so now, in presence of the still surviving Israel, our Wandering Jew, the amended cry was anew taken up, by a succeeding generation of unfortunates, "An honorable scar, your honor, received at Corunna, or at Waterloo, or at Trafalgar!" Yet not a few of these petitioners had never been outside of the London smoke; a sort of crafty aristocracy in their way, who, without having endangered their own persons much if anything, reaped no insignificant share both of the glory and profit of the bloody battles they claimed; while some of the genuine working heroes, too brave to beg, too cut-up to work, and too poor to live, laid down quietly in corners and died. And here it may be noted, as a fact nationally characteristic, that however desperately reduced at times, even to the sewers, Israel, the American, never sunk below the mud, to actual beggary.

Though henceforth elbowed out of many a chance threepenny job by the added thousands who contended with him against starvation, nevertheless, somehow he continued to subsist, as those tough old oaks of the cliffs, which, though hacked at by hail-stones of tempests, and even wantonly maimed by the passing woodman, still, however cramped by rival trees and fettered by rocks,

succeed, against all odds, in keeping the vital nerve of
the tap-root alive. And even towards the end, in his
dismallest December, our veteran could still at intervals
feel a momentary warmth in his topmost boughs. In his
Moorfields' garret, over a handful of reignited cinders
(which the night before might have warmed some lord),
cinders raked up from the streets, he would drive away
dolor, by talking with his one only surviving, and now
motherless child—the spared Benjamin of his old age—
of the far Canaan beyond the sea; rehearsing to the lad
those well-remembered adventures among New England
hills, and painting scenes of nestling happiness and plenty,
in which the lowliest shared. And here, shadowy as it
was, was the second alleviation hinted of above.

To these tales of the Fortunate Isles of the Free, re-
counted by one who had been there, the poor enslaved
boy of Moorfields listened, night after night, as to the
stories of Sinbad the Sailor. When would his father
take him there ? "Some day to come, my boy," would
be the hopeful response of an unhoping heart. And
"Would God it were to-morrow !" would be the impas-
sioned reply.

In these talks Israel unconsciously sowed the seeds of
his eventual return. For with added years, the boy felt
added longing to escape his entailed misery, by compass-
ing for his father and himself a voyage to the Promised
Land. By his persevering efforts he succeeded at last,
against every obstacle, in gaining credit in the right
quarter to his extraordinary statements. In short, charitably stretching a technical point, the American Consul

finally saw father and son embarked in the Thames for Boston.

It was the year 1826; half a century since Israel, in early manhood, had sailed a prisoner in the Tartar frigate from the same port to which he now was bound. An octogenarian as he recrossed the brine, he showed locks besnowed as its foam. White-haired old Ocean seemed as a brother.

CHAPTER XXVII.

REQUIESCAT IN PACE.

IT happened that the ship, gaining her port, was moored to the dock on a Fourth of July; and half an hour after landing, hustled by the riotous crowd near Faneuil Hall, the old man narrowly escaped being run over by a patriotic triumphal car in the procession, flying a broidered banner, inscribed with gilt letters:

"BUNKER-HILL

1775.

GLORY TO THE HEROES THAT FOUGHT!"

It was on Copps' Hill, within the city bounds, one of the enemy's positions during the fight, that our wanderer found his best repose that day. Sitting down here on a mound in the graveyard, he looked off across Charles River towards the battle-ground, whose incipient monument, at that period, was hard to see, as a struggling sprig of corn in a chilly spring. Upon those heights, fifty years before, his now feeble hands had wielded both

ends of the musket. There too he had received that slit
upon the chest, which afterwards, in the affair with the
Serapis, being traversed by a cutlass wound, made him
now the bescarred bearer of a cross.

For a long time he sat mute, gazing blankly about
him. The sultry July day was waning. His son sought
to cheer him a little ere rising to return to the lodging
for the present assigned them by the ship-captain. "Nay,"
replied the old man, "I shall get no fitter rest than here
by the mounds."

But from this true "Potter's Field," the boy at length
drew him away; and encouraged next morning by a
voluntary purse made up among the reassembled passen-
gers, father and son started by stage for the country of
the Housatonic. But the exile's presence in these old
mountain townships proved less a return than a resurrec-
tion. At first, none knew him, nor could recall having
heard of him. Ere long it was found, that more than
thirty years previous, the last known survivor of his
family in that region, a bachelor, following the example
of three-fourths of his neighbors, had sold out and removed to a distant country in the west; where exactly,
none could say.

He sought to get a glimpse of his father's homestead.
But it had been burnt down long ago. Accompanied by
his son, dim-eyed and dim-hearted, he next went to find
the site. But the roads had years before been changed.
The old road was now browsed over by sheep; the new
one ran straight through what had formerly been orchards. But new orchards, planted from other suckers,

and in time grafted, throve on sunny slopes near by, where blackberries had once been picked by the bushel. At length he came to a field waving with buckwheat. It seemed one of those fields which himself had often reaped. But it turned out, upon inquiry, that but three summers since a walnut grove had stood there. Then he vaguely remembered that his father had sometimes talked of planting such a grove, to defend the neighboring fields against the cold north wind; yet where precisely that grove was to have been, his shattered mind could not recall. But it seemed not unlikely that during his long exile, the walnut grove had been planted and harvested, as well as the annual crops preceding and succeeding it, on the very same soil.

Ere long, on the mountain side, he passed into an ancient natural wood, which seemed some way familiar, and midway in it, paused to contemplate a strange, mouldy pile, resting at one end against a sturdy beech. Though wherever touched by his staff, however lightly, this pile would crumble, yet here and there, even in powder, it preserved the exact look, each irregularly defined line, of what it had originally been—namely, a half-cord of stout hemlock (one of the woods least affected by exposure to the air), in a foregoing generation chopped and stacked up on the spot, against sledging-time, but, as sometimes happens in such cases, by subsequent oversight, abandoned to oblivious decay—type now, as it stood there, of forever arrested intentions, and a long life still rotting in early mishap.

"Do I dream?" mused the bewildered old man, "or

what is this vision that comes to me of a cold, cloudy morning, long, long ago, and I heaving yon elbowed log against the beech, then a sapling? Nay, nay, I cannot be so old."

"Come away, father, from this dismal, damp wood," said his son, and led him forth.

Blindly ranging to and fro, they next saw a man ploughing. Advancing slowly, the wanderer met him by a little heap of ruinous burnt masonry, like a tumbled chimney, what seemed the jams of the fire-place, now aridly stuck over here and there, with thin, clinging, round, prohibitory mosses, like executors' wafers. Just as the oxen were bid stand, the stranger's plough was hitched over sideways, by sudden contact with some sunken stone at the ruin's base.

"There, this is the twentieth year my plough has struck this old hearthstone. Ah, old man,—sultry day, this."

"Whose house stood here, friend?" said the wanderer, touching the half-buried hearth with his staff, where a fresh furrow overlapped it.

"Don't know; forget the name; gone West, though, I believe. You know 'em?"

But the wanderer made no response; his eye was now fixed on a curious natural bend or wave in one of the bemossed stone jambs.

"What are you looking at so, father?"

"'*Father!*' Here," raking with his staff, "*my* father would sit, and here, my mother, and here I, little infant, would totter between, even as now, once again, on the very same spot, but in the unroofed air, I do. The ends meet. Plough away, friend."

Best followed now is this life, by hurrying, like itself, to a close.

Few things remain.

He was repulsed in efforts after a pension by certain caprices of law. His scars proved his only medals. He dictated a little book, the record of his fortunes. But long ago it faded out of print—himself out of being—his name out of memory. He died the same day that the oldest oak on his native hills was blown down.

THE END.

THE AMERICAN EXPERIENCE SERIES

"One of the most exciting and promising new ventures in the field of paperback publishing is the American Experience Series now being brought out by Corinth Books. These new and attractive editions of historic and relatively neglected titles fill out in a unique way some of the byways of our country's past."

Robert R. Kirsch in THE LOS ANGELES TIMES